STRANGE REQUESTS AND COMIC TALES FROM RECORD SHOPS

Graham Jones

STRANGE REQUESTS AND COMIC TALES FROM RECORD SHOPS

Graham Jones

Exclusive Distributors in Europe
Music Sales Limited,
14/15 Berners Street,
London, W1T 3LJ.

Published worldwide by
Proper Music Publishing Limited,
Gateway Business Centre,
Kangley Bridge Road,
London, SE26 5AN.

Typeset by Phoenix Photosetting, Chatham, Kent.
Printed by Gutenberg Press.

A catalogue record for this book is available from the British Library.

Visit Omnibus Press on the web at www.omnibuspress.com

Contents

Foreword

by David Sinclair

ilm premieres can bring out the worst in people; all that red carpet, look at me, VIP hoopla is often a perfect distraction to what takes place on the actual screen. But it wasn't like that at the Ritzy in Brixton, when the makers and producers hosted the world premiere of their music documentary film *Last Shop Standing*, which was followed by a Q&A session with the audience. The film is based on Graham Jones' first book of the same name, which tells of the decline of independent record shops in the face of unassailable competition from the supermarkets and digital downloads. Emotions ran high as one person after another in the packed auditorium stood up, not so much to ask questions as to tell their own stories and salute the film as a truly moving testimonial to a sector of the music industry that has been under relentless siege from all quarters for more than a decade.

For these were the people who own, manage and work in record shops – a dedicated band of diehards who have survived a purge that has decimated their ranks and, even now, has not yet run its course. Like Michael Caine and the last of the troops left defending the garrison at Rorke's Drift in the 1964 film *Zulu*, this gathering of folk has fostered a rare sense of camaraderie during which they have managed to defy the overwhelming odds against them. And they certainly have more than a few battle tales to tell.

So far as I know, there have been no reported instances of assegai-wielding warriors seeking to plunder and pillage the record shops of Britain. But over the years there have been some mightily strange incursions into these wondrous emporiums of recorded sound by some very curious characters. These invaders – otherwise known as customers – have come armed with a stream of requests, enquiries and demands so bizarre as to warrant a book of their own.

Graham Jones, who has probably visited more record shops in Britain than anybody else – and certainly more than anyone will ever get to visit in the future – has acquired a vast collection of stories and anecdotes as told to him by the people who have been (mostly) pleased and sometimes bemused to find themselves stationed behind the shop counter of "the industry of human happiness", as Andrew Loog Oldham (manager to The Rolling Stones) famously called the music business. Everyone knows record shops are great places for music fans to hang out – now possibly more than ever before – but who knew they were such a popular refuge for the weird, the wacky and some of the world's most wonderful misfits?

The announcement at the start of 2013 that the HMV chain was going into administration was another gloomy indication of how vulnerable the music retailing sector remains, and of how much work still lies ahead to preserve what is left of it for the future. At least now, thanks to Graham's stories and the drawings of one of the UK's most renowned cartoonists, Kipper Williams, we can all have a good laugh while the last shops standing sort it out.

January 2013

1

Tales from record shops of today

101 Collectors Records, Farnham – Andy Hibberd

Three enthusiastic lads came into the shop. I engaged them in conversation and it was clear to me that they were real music fans. I have strong views about the way some bands and artists have been hyped up in the media as the 'next big thing', good examples being Duffy, Mika and The Darkness, so I decided to share my opinion.

"Take Radiohead," I said. "They're good, but if you listened to the music press, you'd think they were the best band since The Beatles, and not just another indie guitar band!" The three lads started laughing and with that paid for a large batch of bargain LPs they'd selected from my racks, said how much they'd enjoyed visiting and walked out of the shop.

The next day a photographer friend of mine came into the shop and told me that a popular indie band had been at the college in town for a photo shoot he'd organised and while waiting for their lead singer, Thom Yorke, to join them, they'd decided to check out the local record shop. It was then the penny dropped: the lads I'd been chatting away to the previous day were Jonny Greenwood, Ed O'Brien and Phil Selway. I was reliably informed that the boys from Radiohead had enjoyed calling into my shop and appreciated my views on the media hyping bands, including their own!

* * *

Before I worked in a record shop I had a job at a jewellery store. One day Roger Taylor, the drummer with Queen, walked in with his girlfriend. Roger was sporting long, shaggy hair and true rock star-style shades. Being a big Queen fan, I rushed over to serve him. I found him to be a top bloke who was happy to chat while making a considerable purchase and even finding time to sign an autograph.

When they had left the shop my boss asked, "Who were those two women?" I explained that we'd just served one of the greatest drummers of all time. "Oh!", he replied, "I just thought it was a mother and daughter out shopping!" I never did ask him if he'd had Roger down as the mother or the daughter…!

Acorn Records, Yeovil – Chris Lowe

Customer:	"I would like to buy some string."
Shop:	"Do you mean Sting?"

Customer: "No, it's definitely string."
Shop: "What does String sing?"
Customer: "String doesn't sing – it's for tying up parcels!"

Across The Tracks, Brighton – Al Berwick

I noticed a car had broken down outside the shop; the bonnet was up and the owner was looking at the engine. He eventually came into the shop and I expected him to ask for help. When he did speak, however, I was left open-mouthed: "Have you got a clutch for a Citroen 2CV?" he said. He'd just walked past thousands of CDs and records to reach the counter and yet he still asked me that ridiculous question!

"Sorry mate, I don't," I replied, still in shock.

"Ok," he said, "well, what clutches *do* you have in stock then?"

Andy's Records, Aberystwyth – Andy Davis

One busy, hot summer's Saturday I briefly caught sight of a barefoot, skanky long-haired type, with a leather jacket wrapped around his shoulders. He walked into the shop and past the counter towards the CD racking. A few minutes later I glanced up from my busy counter to see this bloke with one of his filthy feet up on the CD rack, caressing my precious stock with said appendage. Being a tad stressed at the time and a bit of a stroppy sod I shouted across the shop at him: "Oi! Get your smelly feet off my CDs RIGHT NOW!"

Silence descended upon the shop, a silence which was only broken by the man's reply: "But I ain't got no arms, mate!"

I just wanted a huge hole to open up and swallow me.

Badlands, Cheltenham – Phil Jump

As well as being a record shop, we also run the Bruce Springsteen fan club. I noticed a lady searching through the stock – she had a distinct look of disappointment on her face. Eventually she asked me if it was true that we ran Bruce's fan club.

"Yes," I replied.

"Well I can't find a *single* Bruce Forsyth record!" she announced.

* * *

A customer came in to order a record. I asked for his name and was thrilled that the gentleman was in fact Mr Suzi Quatro. I was keen to ask him about life with Suzi and what it was like to be married to a world-famous rock star. The gentleman stopped me in my tracks: he wasn't married to Suzi, he was her number one fan and had changed his name in her honour!

Big Brother Records, Poole – Doug Levermore

I thought 'Big Brother' was a great name when I opened the shop, but over the last 12 years it's caused us big problems as it's the same name as the record label set up in 2000 to release rock band Oasis' material (the name is in reference to the band's guitarist and main songwriter, Noel Gallagher, who is older brother to lead singer Liam).

While having the same name has caused me endless headaches it's also given me some great laughs. I've had fans from all over the world ringing up to speak to one of the brothers, as well as banks and financial institutions bestowing their offers to invest thousands in my company. They seem to lose interest when I tell them I'm a second-hand record shop!

The funniest was a girl who phoned up and referred to me as Noel. She'd met the rock star on a recent Oasis tour and was convinced when I answered the phone that I was the man himself; nothing I could say would change her mind. Eventually she asked me, "Why are you putting on that stupid voice, Noel?" I tried to explain that it was my normal voice. The girl still wouldn't believe me and in the end I had to put the phone down.

Borderline Records, Brighton – Dave Minns

A man came to the counter and asked if I'd seen Mick. "Who is Mick?" I said to the man, who I didn't recall ever seeing in the shop before.

"You know, he's the one who goes out with Robyn."

"Who is Robyn?" I replied.

"She works in the furniture shop."

* * *

Like many record shops we display the empty CD case, which the customer then brings to the counter for the staff to dig out the relevant disc, place it in the case and ring the purchase up on the till.

One day a rather dishevelled man brought a case to the counter, telling me he wanted to buy it – he'd been in the shop the week before and was delighted to find this particular CD, since he'd been searching for it for ages. The only problem was that he'd been skint at the time, so he'd decided to just steal it. He'd been most disappointed to discover the case was empty, and he wanted the CD so much he was now prepared to pay for it. I, of course, chased him out of the shop!

* * *

One day a rather serious looking gentleman came to the counter and asked me for Fido music. I had great fun reeling off suggestions: 'Hound Dog' by

Elvis; 'I Wanna Be Your Dog' by The Stooges; 'Rain Dogs' by Tom Waits; 'How Much Is That Doggie In The Window?' by Patti Page; 'Me And You And A Dog Named Boo' by Lobo; 'Diamond Dogs' by David Bowie...

It was clear I was barking up the wrong tree when the gentleman interrupted to explain that 'Fido' was a traditional music of Portugal. I gently explained that what he was after was *Fado* music.

One of my customers is a huge Beach Boys fan and he told me how he'd queued for two hours at Tower Records in New York to get a Beach Boys album signed by Brian Wilson. By the time he got to the front of the queue he got the impression that Brian was tired and losing interest in the signing session. Still, he asked the legendary musician to sign his album 'To Rupert from Brian'.

After he got the signature Rupert left the shop, delighted. It was only on the way home while sitting on the train that he noticed what the Beach Boy had actually written: 'To Brian from Rupert'. Maybe Brian *had* lost interest by that point, or perhaps he just has a wicked sense of humour!

Bridport Music, Bridport – Piers Garner

One day, a West Country local and his wife asked me for some weird and wonderful CDs. The first two were easy to source and order, but then they proudly announced "Here's one you won't be able to find – Shag Connor & The Carrot Crunchers!"

I hunched over the computer and feverishly began typing while an extremely loud track played over the shop's sound system. Then I looked up and asked, in a voice loud enough to be heard over the music, "What's his first name again?"

"Shag!" shouted the bloke in response, but just as he did, the track ended abruptly and the shop fell quiet. He found himself having to apologise profusely to the customers, who'd turned in shock to stare at this seemingly rude man!

* * *

I was standing at the counter and became aware of a lady shouting from the pavement outside. I ignored her, but the yelling continued and I suddenly realised it was me she was shouting at, so I turned the music down. "Are there any Byrd numbers in there?" was what I heard.

"Well, why don't you come in and have a look?" I replied immediately, but as she seemed reluctant to enter, I walked out to her so we could conduct a more civilised conversation. "Yes," I continued, "we have The Byrds' *Definitive Collection*; there are at least 20 tracks on there – everything you could need."

She looked at me as if I was talking another language. "No… I want Byrd numbers!"

Now getting a little cross, I grabbed the case and started to point out the Byrds' hits on the liner notes.

She then grabbed the free newspaper from the stand outside the shop and, waving it at me, raised her voice. "Will I find bird numbers in here?" she said.

"Bird numbers? I don't understand!"

"Numbers… for birds!" she said. "I've come over from Weymouth on the bus and I want to buy a bird – a budgerigar!"

"Have you tried the pet shop?"

"Yes, but they don't have any birds. Are there any people in here (waves paper again) selling *birds*?

"I have no idea," I said, exasperated, "why don't you just take one and have a look? It's free!"

It transpired that she didn't have her glasses with her so I spent the next 10 minutes going through the *Yellow Pages* in a bid to help her find Bridgeport bird sellers so I could get on with my work! A record shop owner's work is never done.

Dales Records, Tenby – Richie Westmacott

The Dales record shop attracts a lot of holidaymakers, since its based in a coastal resort. One day a customer asked for a copy of the soundtrack to *The Sound Of Music* – the gentleman was visiting from Ireland and he'd be in Tenby for a week. I explained the album wasn't in stock but I was able to order it up from the record company. As long it was in for the following Saturday that would be fine, he replied.

Unfortunately, when I rang in the order it was out of stock at the record company, too. The customer returned on the Wednesday, fully expecting to pick up his beloved album. "Sorry – it hasn't arrived yet," I explained, "but it'll hopefully be in tomorrow." But Thursday's deliveries arrived and still no *Sound Of Music*. I began to dread the visit of what was now becoming a very agitated Irishman. "It should be in tomorrow," I told him, when he popped his head round the door.

"It had better be!" was the response.

When the delivery driver arrived on the Friday I rushed to open his box, praying it would contain the soundtrack. To my great disappointment it wasn't there; my heart sank – I knew that no amount of sugar was going to help this medicine go down.

As soon as the man walked through the door I started to apologise, explaining I had done my best. Predictably he was having none of it and said in no uncertain terms that by failing to provide him with the album I'd ruined his family holiday. Even worse, he announced he was a prominent member of an Irish terrorist organisation and would be coming back to Wales to "blow the shop up." I had no idea *The Sound Of Music* could provoke such passion...!

Derricks Music, Swansea – Christos Stylianou

A customer approached the counter with a CD.

"I shall take this if it will fit in my pocket," he proclaimed. "Why don't you try it and see if it fits?" I replied.

"I would have, but I didn't in case you thought I was stealing it." With that he put the CD in his pocket. "Hooray, it's a perfect fit!" he said, his face beaming with satisfaction, "I'll take it."

The next day he came back to the shop. "Did you enjoy the CD?" I asked.

"Don't know," he replied, "it fell out of my pocket before I got home. Can I buy another one please?"

* * *

We've organised lots of personal appearances over the years with many top rock stars, but nothing could compare with the day Welsh easy listening singing star Dorothy Squires did an in-store signing to promote her new album. She was also famed for her marriage to James Bond actor Roger Moore, so when the time came, she attracted a huge crowd that snaked 100 yards down the street. She was funny and charming to all her fans and when we asked her if she would like a cup of tea she replied, "Oh no dear, I need something much stronger – a whiskey will do." We had to nip out and buy a bottle as we didn't normally keep hard liquor in the record shop!

Europa Music, Stirling – Ewan Duncan

Customer:	"I'm looking for Loo Rolls."
Shop:	"Don't you mean Lou Rawls?"
Foreign male customer:	"I'm looking for Dido."
Shop:	"We have all her albums in stock."
Customer:	"Can I see them?"
Shop:	"Of course!" (I proceeded to gather up Dido's albums).
Customer:	"Oh no! I was looking a for long rubber thing!"
Shop:	"Try Ann Summers round the corner…"

Head Records, Leamington Spa – Simon Dullenty

Customer:	"Have you got that Shhhssshhh song?"

After many questions and with the customer looking at me as if I was an idiot I discovered he was actually after Bjork singing 'It's Oh So Quiet'.

* * *

Another customer asked us if we'd any gypsy pole-dancing DVDs. Now that conjures up a strange image in your mind!

Kingbee Records, Manchester – Les Hare

We originally opened with a market stall in Chorlton. I took on a young indie music fan called Rosie to help out. On Wednesday afternoons I would leave her in charge and take a tour around the other Manchester record shops to gauge the musical temperature and pick up a few bargains.

Left to her own devices, a mischievous Rosie would constantly play The Smiths album *Meat Is Murder*, the title track of which was written by militant vegetarian and Smiths lead singer Morrissey. The record finishes with the disturbing sound of cattle on their way to the abattoir.

I would get back on Thursday mornings to angry complaints from the butcher's stall across the way. They'd ask Rosie to turn off the music, but instead she'd turn up the volume, causing distress to the old ladies queuing up to buy their sausages and pies to the awful sounds of the unfortunate cattle waiting to be turned into steak.

*   *   *

Every day we'd see a strange lady walking past the shop dressed from head to toe in purple. We often wondered where she was going and why she only dressed in the one colour. We christened her 'Purple Woman' because of her eccentric appearance.

One day she came into the shop and we waited with anticipation to hear the 'Purple Woman' speak. She pointed at a picture disc on the wall. "I'd like that record please." The album in question was Prince's *Purple Rain*. I pointed out that it was £30, but it didn't matter; 'Purple Woman' was buying it. She left the shop and has never called in since.

She still walks by most days and I'm always on the look-out for more purple-related records to hang in the window in the hope of enticing her back in. So far I've tried Deep Purple and Hendrix's 'Purple Haze', but I've had no luck with either.

*   *   *

One of my most memorable customers was the man who was spending an eternity browsing through the racks, much to the annoyance of his impatient partner who just wanted him to decide what he wanted so they could leave.

It was clear he was getting annoyed with his partner's nagging and after a heated exchange he agreed to go. He brought his selections to the counter and I totalled up his purchases, his partner still haranguing him as they left the shop.

I could see the disagreement was carrying on outside when suddenly the man turned around and came back in. "I forgot one thing!" he announced to everybody in earshot. He then proceeded to bring a Smiths poster to the till. "I'll take this 'Girlfriend In A Coma' poster, please." Hopefully that wasn't the shape of things to come…!

Les Aldrich, London – Mark Daniel

We have a record shop in Muswell Hill that stocks most types of music. The one section we don't stock widely is French music, much to the displeasure of one customer. The man in question registered his disappointment, mistaking the shop to be a French music specialist. How could he have made such an error? It was all in the name: Les (or as pronounced in French, 'lay') Aldrich

Lewks, Downham Market – Lawrence Welham

A lady called in, asking for 'the Anna Neagle song'. Anna was a famous English actress who was very popular during the war years, but she'd also had some success as a singer in the Thirties. I looked up her recordings and started reading them out to the lady but none of them rang a bell with her. "Would it help if I sang the song I am after?" she said.

"Yes," I replied, "I'm sure I will recognise it if you sing it." Off she went: *"Did you ever know that you're my hero and everything I would like to be? I can fly higher than Anna Eagle, because you are the wind beneath my wings."*

I can no longer hear the lyrics from Bette Midler's 'Wind Beneath My Wings' without thinking of the the wartime actress and that mistaken fan…!

* * *

One very posh lady asked if we had a DVD of the Theekers. Assuming she had a speech impediment I showed her a DVD of the 1960s Australian band The Seekers, fronted by Judith Durham, and told her it featured all the hits, including 'The Carnival Is Over,' 'Georgy Girl' and 'I'll Never Find Another You.'

It turned out the lady didn't have a speech problem at all – what she was after was a film about a family of the same name.

Suddenly, I got an idea. "Do you mean *Meet The Fockers?*" I asked. "Yes, that's it – I didn't wish to say that title!"

*   *   *

A teenager came in and asked for the new rap CD by John Paul. I guessed that the Polish pope, who'd occupied the Vatican from 1978 until his death in 2005, hadn't produced a rap album and suggested that it might be Sean Paul, the rapper, he was after...

Customer: "Do you have any batteries?"
Shop: "We don't stock them but try the supermarket down the road."

> Customer: "I don't wish to buy *batteries*, I want a CD of 'The
>   Batteries'."

I presumed they were an indie band that I hadn't heard of and started researching. I asked the man if he had any more information, to which he replied, "Well, I know they are Irish and were big in the Sixties." That's when the penny dropped! I guess 'The Batteries' was easy to confuse with The Bachelors, the Sixties hit pop group.

* * *

A very well spoken and immaculately dressed elderly gentleman called into the shop asking for 'clear' CDs. Having been asked for 'clear tapes' over the years, which we always took to mean blank tapes, I guessed what he really meant was blank CDs, so asked if he wanted them for recording music.

"Well no, not really," he replied, before asking to take a look at some of the blank CDs I had in stock.

"Perhaps you mean blank DVDs?" I enquired, which again brought the same response.

"Well no, not really!" He was obviously reluctant to explain further what he intended to use them for.

Thinking he might in fact be trying to back up computer data, I asked if that was his reason for wanting them.

Again came the response. "Well no, not really!"

"Perhaps transferring pictures from a digital camera to a computer?"

"Well no, not really!"

Sensing I wasn't getting anywhere I changed tack. "Are you going to use the discs in a computer?"

"Well no, not really!" he repeated.

"In a recorder to store TV programmes so you can watch them later?

"Well no, not really!"

"In a CD recorder so you can listen to music later?"

"Well no, not really... I actually want them to scare away pigeons!" He then went on to clarify the matter "I string them up and as they blow in the wind they keep the pigeons off my crops. I've already bought some cheap CDs from a charity shop, but they're only silver on one side, with a printed label on the other, and they don't work as well as the ones which are shiny on both sides."

That was a new one to me but we happily supplied him with 10 silver blank CDs, without cases, as there really didn't seem to be a need for them.

We did wonder how he'd discovered that pigeons aren't bothered by CDs with printed labels on one side: had he done some in-depth interviews with the local flock? I'm now going to offer to do a presentation for our local Young Farmers' club to see if they might be interested in this idea on a commercial scale – if I can get some of the local cereal farmers with huge fields interested I shall seize the opportunity to grow my blank CD market!

Moondance Music & Video, Waltham Cross – Ergun Ahmed

Customer: "Have you got a CD by U2?"

Shop: I looked at my assistant and announced "Nope, we've never made a CD together."

*   *   *

A man walked up to the counter and asked if I had two brothers. I was amazed and confirmed that, in fact, I did; one lives in London and the other in Colchester. After I'd gone into detail about what my brothers were now up to I asked him how he'd known about them. "I didn't!" he replied, "I'm after a DVD of the film *Two Brothers*!" It turned out he'd been after the 2004 film starring Guy Pearce, about two tiger cubs who are separated and reunited years later.

Mound Music, Edinburgh – Dougie Anderson

American customer: "Hi! Do you have any CDs by Stella Jones?"

Shop: "I'll just check our computer database for you."

After searching for a few minutes with no luck I said that since I recognised from the customer's voice that she was American, I'd check the USA database as well in case Stella had released something there. After a few minutes' fruitless searching, I gave up. "I'm sorry but there's nothing listed worldwide for Stella Jones. If you tell me what radio station you heard her on I can contact them and get the details?"

"Oh, I never heard her on the radio!" the American replied. "I sat next to her in high school 20 years ago and she had the most amazing voice. I was convinced that she would have made a CD by now!"

*   *   *

We definitely had the least knowledgeable Beatles fan visit the shop. She'd come in asking where she should try to sell a signed Beatles LP. "It's not signed by John Lennon, but it *is* signed by the other three – Paul McCartney, Ringo Starr and Rex Harrison."

*   *   *

One day, a rather excited gentleman asked for a CD out of the window. He explained that it'd be a perfect gift for his friends but before he purchased it he'd like to have a quick listen. I was happy to oblige and put the disc on the player; it was called *Heather And Glen* and was a collection of Scottish folk songs and music from Aberdeenshire and the Hebrides, collected by the celebrated musicologist Alan Lomax. After a few minutes I noticed the man didn't seem to really appreciate the music and it was no surprise when he told me his friends wouldn't like the album. Keen to obtain a sale I asked him what sort of music they *did* like – if he was looking for a gift we would surely stock something suitable. "Not unless it's called Glenn and Heather, the names of my friends!" he replied.

*   *   *

The shop is popular with tourists looking to take home traditional Scottish music, but it's fair to say we've had a few encounters with eccentric customers. One tourist phoned in after reading on the Internet that the shop was perched high above Princes Street in Edinburgh.

Customer: "Can you tell me how high you are?"
Shop: "Me or the shop?"

Customer: "The shop."

Shop: "About 10 metres!"

Customer: "No, you don't understand: I need to know what altitude you're at as I'd like to visit but I'm prone to altitude sickness!"

*   *   *

Customer: "I'd like to buy this Sandy Denny box set, but as you have the Internet could you check who is the cheapest?"

Muse Music, Hebden Bridge – Sid Jones

Customer: "I'm after a Who CD but it must contain the track about the deaf, dumb and blind boy who sure plays a mean trombone."

Shop: "The track is 'Pinball Wizard' but the deaf, dumb and blind boy sure plays a mean *pinball*!"

Music Memorabilia, Alfriston – Robert Deval

An old traditional accordion took pride of place in my window display. One day the police called round carrying an accordion that looked very similar to mine and asked me if I recognised it. I looked at the shop window – my accordion had gone and I hadn't even noticed. I asked the officers how they'd come into the possession of my beloved instrument.

"Well sir, we stopped a gentleman and when we asked him to get out of his car we noticed your accordion on the back seat. We asked him if it was his and how long he'd owned it. He said he'd had it for ages as he made his living as a busker. We became suspicious as it still had a price tag attached showing your shop name. We asked him to play us a tune, so he reluctantly agreed to show us his busking skills. Sadly, the sound he made was more like a pack of wailing cats! He knew the game was up and confessed to stealing it from your shop, so we're here to return it."

Music's Not Dead, Bexhill-on-Sea – Del Querns

One charming customer came in, had a good look around, approached the counter and announced loudly, "Your shop, mate, is right up its own arse!"

Piccadilly Records, Manchester – Philippa Jarmen

We are known for stocking cutting edge, independent music but originally we also sold pop records. It was when a sales rep sold a Paul Young album to us that we learned not to always trust what a rep tells you. His tactic was to tell us that unless he hit his sales target and achieved his bonus, he'd have to sell his daughter's pony and he didn't wish to break her heart. We fell for this sob story and gave him a massive order. Years later we were still selling the surplus Paul Young CDs, eventually reducing them to 10p each. On the plus side, on the rare occasion we sold a copy we consoled ourselves with the fact the pony was safe!

The Stone Roses' bass player Mani walked up to the counter wearing dungarees, a pair of yellow waders and a hard hat, while in his hands was a chainsaw. He plonked the scary piece of machinery on the counter as if it wasn't anything out of the ordinary and asked if Miles Davis' *Bitches Brew* was in stock. He left a happy man, with Miles Davis' album in one hand, the chainsaw in the other.

Probe Records, Liverpool – Geoff Davis

To supplement my takings in the early days of the record shop, I decided to enter the world of gig promotion. I was a huge fan of a new band from the north-east called Roxy Music who had yet to break through into the big time. I was keen to put them on in Liverpool and when their agent asked if we had anything available I let my enthusiasm get the better of my judgment and offered to book them as a support to a gig I was putting on.

At Liverpool Stadium, Bryan Ferry and company took to the stage to support Nazareth and Rory Gallagher, whose fans tended to be diehard rockers, i.e. people who didn't have much in common with the band's glam rock glittery clothes and make-up. They of course proceeded to boo and heckle the band.

After the gig a despondent Bryan Ferry told me he needed a drink. Back in the late Seventies pubs in Liverpool had their last orders at 10.30 p.m. and I realised they wouldn't get to a pub in time but told Bryan I knew somewhere they could get an after-hours drink – the Nigerian social club. As the band entered they realised the club was inhabited by some rough looking characters. I sat them down at a table while I went to get the beers. With their flamboyant clothes, the band stood out like the Blackpool illuminations and attracted much interest from the club's regular clientele. Bryan smiled as two ladies approached the table, assuming they were fans of the band – in fact, they were prostitutes touting for business! I noticed the fear in Ferry and Brian Eno's eyes and they started gulping their pints down as if they were in a rush to leave. As soon as they finished their drinks they thanked me and set off back to their hotel. I'm sure the lads from Roxy Music have never forgotten their first Liverpool gig!

*   *   *

Strange Requests And Comic Tales From Record Shops

The year 1976 was an epic one for Probe as we moved into a building in Rainford Gardens that was to become iconic. I'd taken the advice of Eric's club owner and friend Roger Eagle and moved the premises to a more central location near his club – this was a shrewd move; it coincided with the punk explosion and our shop became central to the mushrooming 'Eric's scene' that gave birth to scores of Liverpool punk rock bands. We were just off Mathew Street, less than a minutes' walk from Eric's, so the shop became a meeting place for followers of this new movement. The night before the opening the staff were still busy painting and varnishing in an attempt to get everything ready. Around 9 p.m. I announced that I was going to Eric's to watch one of my favourite bands, The Flamin' Groovies, and despite the painting being nowhere near finished the staff downed tools and joined me. After the gig I was talking with the band and told them we'd given up painting the shop to come and see them play. I explained that we must get back to finish the job and to my astonishment the band came back to help. So, with the help of The Flamin' Groovies – who stayed painting till 3 a.m. – we opened the next day!

* * *

Some of the people who helped behind the counter at Probe included Julian Cope of The Teardrop Explodes, Pete Wylie of Wah! and Paul Rutherford of Frankie Goes to Hollywood fame, but our most notorious assistant was Pete Burns, who was later to find success as the singer with the pop band Dead or Alive, who achieved a number one single in 1985 with 'You Spin Me Round (Like A Record)'. Pete had started work at the shop after his wife, Lynne, had also landed a job with us, the difference being that while Lynne would arrive on time for opening, Pete would stroll in around 1 p.m.

Pete became famous for letting customers know when he didn't approve of their musical taste, always done with his trademark caustic wit.

One hot summer's evening I had just settled down with a spliff when the phone rang – it was Pete and he sounded quite agitated; he asked me if I could come and get him out of his flat as a riot was going on outside. It turned out to be the beginning of what would become the Toxteth riots: this was Margaret Thatcher's Britain and the country was divided between rich and poor – the people of Toxteth certainly felt they belonged to the latter category. At the time, the Merseyside police had a poor reputation within the black community thanks to the policy of stopping and searching young black men. The hot sticky weather on July 3 only added to the tense atmosphere, while the perceived heavy-handed arrest of Leroy Alphonse Cooper in front of an already agitated crowd was the spark that ignited the fire, seemingly right outside Pete's flat.

Thanks to the spliff I was in no state to drive but sensing Pete was in danger I set off, aiming to bring him back to my house. As I approached the turning into Pete's road I drove into a scene from *Spartacus*! Rioters were attacking the police with sticks and staves while the police fought back with truncheons. I quickly reversed and tried to reach Pete by going on a detour to his back door, but as I turned the corner I was met by a wild mob throwing bricks and stones, many heading in my direction – I was stoned but also literally stoned! I parked my car up and rushed into Pete's flat.

When I got inside we realised that we couldn't escape so we locked the door and went upstairs to watch the riot from the balcony. We had the best view but watched in horror as the police lost control. Cars were being set alight and the local Kwik Save store had their windows smashed so people poured in and helped themselves to the alcohol. The Rialto Ballroom, a venue that The Beatles had played many times, was set alight.

In all, the rioting lasted nine days, during which one person died (after being struck by a police vehicle trying to clear crowds), 468 police officers were injured, over 500 people were arrested and at least 70 buildings were damaged so severely by fire that they had to be demolished. Around a hundred cars were destroyed, although amazingly not my old banger, which I recovered the next day. The drive back to the shop was surreal as we knew the area so well and so many landmarks were now just burnt-out shells.

Raves from the Grave, Frome – Richard Churchyard

A very excited customer brought a record to the counter. "Wow! I've been looking everywhere for this – I can't believe I've found it at last!" he said. Two minutes later we asked if he'd like to pay for it, to which he replied "I think I'll leave it for now."

Record Collector, Sheffield – Barry Everard

I decided to celebrate the fact that the shop in Broomhill was 33⅓ years old (being a record shop), so to commemorate the occasion I threw a party. Friends promised they would line up a special act for the night and on the day of the party I still had no idea who the mystery band would be. The event, which was billed as 'A Tribute to Barry Everard', was featured on local radio and the press informed potential attendees that there'd be a nominal £2 entrance fee.

The night was a great success but there must be hundreds of music fans in Sheffield who regret not attending as the secret band turned out to be Richard Hawley and Martin Simpson; it was the first time two of Sheffield's finest sons had appeared as a duo. Those who witnessed this gig, which has taken on a mythical status, will never forget it.

The event also led to a funny incident the next day. I was walking through town when a man I recognised as a customer, approached me. When he noticed me the colour drained from his face, leaving it white as a sheet. He stuttered. "Barry is that you?"

"Er, yes!" I replied.

"What are you doing here?" the man asked.

"I'm just going to my shop."

"But aren't you dead? I read in the paper they were having a tribute night for you!"

I politely explained that I was clearly still going, and so was the shop – at 33⅓, it was doing just fine.

*　　*　　*

While sorting out all my old newspaper cuttings I came across a flyer advertising a gig I'd sold tickets for back in 1980; it was at The Marples pub and the headliner was Nico, the German-born singer and actress who found fame with the Velvet Underground and whose solo album *Chelsea Girl*, released in 1967, is regarded as a cult classic. I thought my customers would find the flyer of interest, so I put it in the shop window. A few minutes later a lady came in, purchased a couple of CDs and then asked for two tickets to the Nico concert. It didn't occur to her that £2 was extremely cheap for a gig, but even more amazing is she was unaware that Nico was tragically killed in a cycling accident in 1988 so definitely would not be appearing. I decided it was probably best to take the flyer down and put it back into storage…!

* * *

One of our regular customers is 'Van the Man' who acquired the nickname as he would come into the shop, often after a few drinks, and stand by the counter talking about his hero Van Morrison, Van's great albums and the concerts he had seen him perform over the years. One day 'Van the Man' was staggering around the shop more inebriated than ever, not seeming to know where he was. His condition was causing a bit of concern among the staff. "What's wrong with 'Van the Man'?" asked my assistant.

"He's just suffering from 'Alkie–zheimers!" was my reply.

* * *

Customer: "Music is my religion and this shop is my church."

* * *

It's fair to say that I'm not a great fan of modern technology and a reluctant user of the Internet. The shop is based near Sheffield University and one day I was talking to a student who asked if I was on Twitter.

"No!" I replied.

"I guess you're not a fan of the Twittersphere then," commented the student.

"You're right, but I am a fan of the 'Talkersphere' though, as I like to talk to people!" was my response.

* * *

Customer: "You know when people die they sometimes have their
             ashes thrown on the pitch of their favourite football team?"
Shop: "Yes…"
Customer: "When I die I'd like to be buried under your shop."
Shop: "Oh!"

* * *

Customer: "Have you got the song about the transsexual who nearly misses the train?"

Shop: "I guess you're after 'Last Train To Transcentral' by the KLF."

*   *   *

On a similar theme, a shop owner based in a seaside town told me this tale about one of his best customers, but for reasons that will become clear he asked if I wouldn't name the shop and change the names of those involved.

Being based in a seaside town, Paul, the owner of the shop, has a high number of customers who only visit once a year during their holidays. One such person was Colin, who during his annual pilgrimage would spend a lot of time in the shop while his wife took the children to the beach. Every visit would end with him purchasing a selection of CDs, as if he couldn't leave the shop without buying something. Paul enjoyed Colin's visits, not just because he spent so much money, but it was fun to swap tales with a fellow music fanatic.

However, after fifteen years, Colin stopped calling in. Paul presumed that perhaps he'd decided to take his holidays somewhere else or maybe he was struggling financially and could no longer afford his annual trip to the seaside.

A few years later, Paul received a phone call out of the blue from his old mate who said that he was visiting the following week and would be calling into the shop to stock up on CDs. Paul was delighted and told Colin that he was looking forward to seeing him again. Just as he was about to put the phone down Colin said, "Paul, I have something to tell you... my name is no longer Colin, it's Coleen... " For the next few minutes Coleen proceeded to tell Paul how he was now living as a woman before undergoing gender reassignment surgery. He also said how pleased he was with his new look and challenged Paul to see if he could recognise him when he called in.

For the next few days Paul peered at every woman who came into the shop, trying to decipher if it was his old mate Colin, now Coleen. He needn't have worried about missing her as on a sunny afternoon a tall lady in shades teetered into the shop. Paul wasn't sure if it was the badly fitted wig, the poorly applied make-up, the short skirt that looked more suitable for a teenager or the high heels she struggled to walk in that gave it away. For the next few minutes he tried to decide what he should say to his friend; he was conscious of not wanting to hurt Coleen's feelings so when the lady came to the counter with a selection of CDs he chirped up with "Hi Col, my old mate, you look fantastic! It was only the way you walk in the high heels that gave it away!"

"Pardon?" the person replied, in a very feminine voice.

To Paul's horror it wasn't Coleen standing in front of him, just a badly dressed lady. He could feel his face turning a bright shade of pink, his brain locked, his mouth dried up, and he couldn't think of a word to say. For the next few seconds there was a deathly silence and Paul's face went from pink to cerise!

Eventually the woman broke the quiet, "Did you think I was a man?"

"Um, no, I thought you were a friend of mine called Coleen," replied Paul.

"But you called me 'mate' and said it was the high heels that gave me away!"

Paul had no reply and more silence followed as his face now took on the colour of a deep purple.

The lady turned on her high heels, calling Paul a very rude man, and exited the shop, leaving the potential purchase of CDs sitting on the counter.

The next day another person came into the shop with an ill-fitting wig, poorly applied make-up, a dress far too short and heels much too high. Paul knew straightaway that it was Coleen, but his confidence was shattered by the previous days' encounter, so when his friend brought her purchase to the counter he stayed silent. As soon as he shut the till Coleen said enthusiastically, "Paul, it's me Coleen – I told you you wouldn't recognise me!"

Reflex, Newcastle-upon-Tyne – Alan Jordan

We used to sell concert tickets and organise coach trips to see bands. The day after Kurt Cobain sadly committed suicide I received this phone call.

Customer: "Hi, I bought tickets for the coach trip to see Nirvana in Manchester. I was just wondering if the trip was still going ahead?"

Rise Music, Bristol – Gordon Montgomery

The first record shop I owned was below a Chinese restaurant; a few days before Christmas its toilets flooded, resulting in water and urine seeping through the ceiling. When I turned up the following morning I realised something wasn't quite right – we always display the latest releases in plastic LP covers in the shop window and as I got nearer I became aware that they looked swollen, like the bags you get at a fairground when you win a goldfish, except the water wasn't crystal clear but a pale yellow! It was a total disaster – I had to throw out hundreds of damaged CDs and vinyl and spent the day trying to banish the smell of sewage from the shop.

The Rock Box, Camberley – Ken Dudley

One of our best customers was a fanatical fan of anarchic punk band Crass and was involved with a fanzine called *The Green Anarchist*, an extreme left-wing magazine which was supportive of the Animal Liberation Front. I was happy to sell the fanzine in the shop for him.

One day he asked if it would be OK to have his mail delivered to The Rock Box, as his parents weren't too happy with the anarchic work he was doing. "Of course, no problem!" I said. Later, these words would come back to haunt me.

It turned out this guy was involved in disrupting the start of the 1993 Grand National horse race. Soon afterwards, I was paid a visit by two menacing looking characters who wanted a word with 'The Green Anarchist'. I explained that he didn't live on the premises and he simply used the shop as a postal address. But it was clear they didn't believe me, especially when they told me to make sure nobody was in the building that evening as the premises would be firebombed. As they left they tore down posters from the wall. I decided it best to go to the local police and report the incident. They took me very seriously and that night decided to install cameras and stake out the shop.

In the early hours the cameras picked up on a thick-set skinhead carrying a bag and approaching the shop door. Tension was high as they waited to see what he would do next. As he reached the door he stuffed something through the letterbox before moving off. The police quickly intercepted the item only to discover it wasn't a firebomb at all, but a leaflet saying 'VOTE BNP'!

It was just a BNP member campaigning for the forthcoming election. Luckily I never heard from the threatening characters again, although I did ask The Green Anarchist to get his post delivered elsewhere!

* * *

A regular customer in the shop's early days was Queen guitarist Brian May. He would often call in with his son, who was a big fan of rap music (clearly having one of the greatest guitarists of all time for a dad didn't influence his musical taste!). Brian always paid by cheque – I reckon some shops would have kept those cheques as a souvenir rather than banking them!

RPM Music, Newcastle-upon-Tyne – Marek Norvid

A man who had clearly been indulging in a little too much alcohol came into the shop one day. He approached the counter and asked if we could tattoo his arm. We politely explained that he was in a record shop and the tattoo parlour was next door.

One week later the same, slightly drunk gentleman came in and again asked if we could give him a tattoo – again we explained that he needed to go next door.

The whole episode happened again the following week, so the next time I saw him stagger in I shouted "The tattooist is next door mate!"

"It's OK," he replied, "I'm not after a tattoo today – I need a taxi to the station!"

* * *

We had a listening post with four sets of headphones, which allowed customers to test out CDs before they bought them. One regular customer would visit every week with his Alsatian dog in tow. He was always interested in the new releases so he'd make use of our listening post: one set of headphones for himself and another for the dog. If the dog howled then its owner wouldn't buy the CD but if the dog remained silent he would!

Seedee Jons, Jersey – Jon Holley

When we first opened the shop we thought it would be a good idea to have 12 television screens simultaneously showing MTV. One day there were problems with MTV so we showed Channel 4 Racing instead. Next thing we know a drunk wanders in and, mistaking us for a bookies, asks for a betting slip!

Skeleton Records, Birkenhead – John Weaver/Andy Jones

I must be the only man to have booked the Sex Pistols three times and even though every gig was cancelled, I still managed to make a profit. On the first two occasions it was the band that cancelled, but I was able to rearrange a replacement gig. I hired out a large cabaret club in Birkenhead called The Hamilton; recent performers included Tom O'Connor, Tony Christie, Stan Boardman and The Grumbleweeds – it was the sort of place that served chicken in a basket with a raffle after the first act, hardly the place you would expect the most controversial band in the country to perform.

On the day the tickets were put on sale I had more than 80 people queuing outside the shop. By the end of that day every ticket had sold for what was to become the most anticipated gig in Birkenhead's history.

But before I knew it the Hamilton Club started to get pressure from both the council and the police to cancel the gig, something they had never experienced while putting on Tom O'Connor! Things got even worse when the Sex Pistols started the tour: stories of the band's antics, which were corrupting the youth of the nation, dominated the pages of the tabloids. The owners decided ("with much reluctance"), had to cancel the gig. It was devastating news for me and I braced myself for hundreds of fans coming in to the shop to claim a refund. But the rush never materialised and throughout the day only a trickle of fans came in to ask for their money back. It was clear the others kept their unused tickets as souvenirs, helping me to an £800 profit on a gig that never happened!

One extremely busy Saturday an aggravating little chap bounded over to the counter and asked "D'ya wanna buy some jazz?"

"You'll have to see John, the owner, as he does the buying," my assistant, Andy, replied.

But a queue of people looking to sell records to me did not deter the annoying little sod from pushing to the front and growling "D'ya wanna buy some jazz?"

I didn't take kindly to this and snarled back "There's a queue, you'll have to wait!"

For his next move, he rushed back to Andy "Don't you want some jazz for yourself?"

Andy repeated that since he didn't do the buying, he'd have to wait until I'd finished dealing with the other customers who were themselves waiting patiently to sell their wares.

The young lad then proceeded to approach the customers: "D'ya wanna buy any jazz?"

By this time Andy was wondering what was in the bag – Charlie Parker, Bessie Smith or perhaps a bit of John Coltrane? Eventually he asked the lad to show him: the great unveiling took place, only for the contents to be six bottles of Yves Saint Laurent Jazz aftershave (no doubt missing from Superdrug down the road)!

*   *   *

A man came in and asked for the song about hopping – straight away I realised he wasn't after hopping, but hoping, The Merseybeats' 1964 hit 'Wishin' And Hopin''.

Slipped Discs, Billericay – Carl Newsum

One female customer told me that the Nickelback CD she'd purchased was jumping and she wanted a replacement. "Of course!" I replied, "I'll send it back to the record company and they'll refund me, providing I can give them some details of why you're returning it – do you know which track it jumps on and at what time?"

"Yes," replied the lady, "it jumps on track six and I remember looking up at the clock when I was listening to it, so it was about five past eleven."

* * *

A man came in and asked if we had any 'Chitchat'. Like most people, I'm perfectly happy with a bit of small talk and not being familiar with his request, I asked the man if 'Chitchat' was a band. "Yes," he replied.

I laughed to myself, as I thought I'd worked out why he'd got confused. "Do you mean Talk Talk?" I asked confidently.

"No, it is definitely Chitchat!"

It took a while, but I eventually realised that he was actually after Eighties jazz-funk band Shakatak (that was one of my better bits of detective work)!

* * *

My most memorable customer was 'Lycra Lorraine', so named because she popped into the shop after her weekly trip to the gym wearing a pink Lycra catsuit. Each week she'd spend over an hour in the shop asking me for my recommendations, often spending over a hundred pounds. It was obvious that she was wealthy as she'd regularly go on long holidays but she would stay in touch by letter, asking me what releases were out and writing how much she looked forward to coming back into the shop.

One day I commented that I hadn't eaten and she suggested I could go back to her house after work and she'd cook me something good. Later my assistant suggested that it wasn't perhaps the music 'Lycra Lorraine' was keen on, but me! I believed this to be preposterous but the more I thought about it the more I realised my assistant might be right. I didn't want to lose a customer but decided the next time Lorraine came in I would slip on my wedding ring. When she noticed the ring on my finger, a look of disappointment washed over her face and she left without purchasing anything.

I didn't see Lorraine for a couple of years until she turned up to ask if we would buy her large record collection. When I said I couldn't give her much for it she reminded me I'd been the one to recommend them in the first place. Clearly 'Lycra Lorraine' was no longer a music fan!

Soul Brother Records, Putney – Laurence Prangell

Soul Brother is not just a shop; we often arrange gigs and signings on the premises.

One artist we did this for was Leroy Burgess. Leroy had been a member of Seventies R&B band Black Ivory before going on to have his own successful solo career.

We'd arranged to drive Leroy between venues and his hotel in London and on the day of the first gig we asked him if he fancied going for a bite to eat. He asked how far it was to the Kings Road, as last time he'd been in the UK he'd eaten at a fabulous place that served the most amazing beef rolls. Kings Road wasn't too far away so I asked him what the place was called.

"Tesco Extra," he replied.

Of all the fantastic places in London we could have eaten, I found myself in Leroy's hotel room tucking into rolls from the supermarket. And the next two nights followed suit as Leroy only fancied eating from the same place. He was delighted to hear that Tesco Extra had shops all over the UK so if he ever did a nationwide tour he could pick up his beloved rolls anywhere.

This wasn't the last time Soul Brother would have fun with an American soul star and their food. Marlena Shaw, who had achieved success on the Blue Note record label, was brought over to the UK to promote an anthology released on our own Soul Brother record label. We really pushed the boat out, hiring a Bentley complete with chauffeur to drive her between promotional appearances. Looking every inch the star, Marlena asked the driver to pull over near a row of shops. A few minutes later she emerged in her glamorous outfit and got back into the Bentley with a bucket of KFC. An argument then followed as the chauffeur wasn't keen on her eating the fried chicken in his spotless vehicle! Eventually they reached a compromise and the chauffeur drove Marlena back to her hotel so she could tuck into her deep-fried feast in the comfort of her room!

* * *

One of our favourite artists is George Clinton, and we have fond memories of his whirlwind visit to the shop. He burst in, barefoot and shouting "How you funkin' all?" and then went on to purchase dozens of albums. But even he caused us problems.

George was playing at the Shepherd's Bush Empire and Soul Brother was selling the merchandise. The gig was a sell-out and we were looking forward to doing brisk business at the end of George's performance. But herein lay the problem: George took to the stage at 8 p.m. and over four hours later he was still playing; it looked like his show was never going to end! Eventually the management turned all the lights off but that didn't stop George, he just kept on going. A few minutes later the plug was pulled and security had to remove George from the stage. With security shepherding the audience out by the light of their mobile phones they all walked straight past the merchandise stall. We'd been there for nearly five hours but hardly took a penny!

Sounds Interesting, Bideford – Brian Ottway

Customer:	"Do you stock Ha Ha?"
Shop:	"I'm sorry, do you mean A-ha?"
Customer:	"No it's definitely Ha Ha. I guess you've not heard of them because they're Norwegian."

* * *

Customer:	"Did I leave my baby in here?" (She had indeed left her baby in the shop – for over 20 minutes!)

Sound Knowledge, Marlborough – Roger Mortimer

I will never forget my first day of trading. I opened the door and proudly informed a man who was waiting to get in that he was the shop's very first customer. "I'm no customer!" the man replied. He told me he was from the Performing Right Society (PRS) and had come to check there was a licence to play music at the premises. The price of a licence varies depending on the type of business premises, but is currently £79 a year for record shops. I had to pay up before I'd sold a single thing!

The next visitor to walk through the door was a gentleman who approached the counter only to tell me that the shop was condemned to failure. "This yard where your shop is has had so many failed businesses that they should change the name from Hughenden Yard to Grave Yard!" he said. I thanked the merchant of doom for his words of wisdom and then asked how I could be of help. "Oh, I've not come down to buy anything – I just thought I'd let you know that you're on to a loser!"

* * *

Dave Hill is the guitarist with Slade, one of the most famous bands of the Seventies. He was great fun, and used to tell the staff many anecdotes from his days in the band and how he'd met George Michael at the airport and chatted away to him for ages until he realised George didn't have a clue who he was talking to. Dave explained that he'd come down to Marlborough to purchase antiques. Later that evening, I was speaking with my brother Andrew who ran a restaurant in the Midlands called Berkeley's, and was regaling him with my Dave Hill tales.

The next day who should walk into my brother's restaurant but none other than Dave Hill! My brother saw his opportunity to have some fun. He asked Dave if he'd enjoyed Wiltshire on his recent trip. He then asked about the antiques Dave had bought. Dave was spooked and couldn't work out how this seemingly psychic waiter knew so much about him!

* * *

Customer: "Have you the new CD by Andrew Marr?"
Shop: (I look up Andrew Marr on the computer to see if the political journalist has recorded anything but it comes up with a blank. Meanwhile the customer is insisting it is Andrew Marr and not only is he a good singer but he is a great dancer, too.) "Is it by any chance Olly Murs?" I ask.
Customer: "That's him!"

* * *

The shop has many famous customers, among them English soccer legend Stuart Pearce, who is a big fan of punk and indie guitar and once introduced his heroes the Sex Pistols onstage at their reunion gig in Finsbury Park.

One day he was in the shop choosing a handful of CDs. I was on the phone to one of the record companies phoning through an order, so Stuart passed his selection to Helen, one of the store's assistants. Stuart had spent over £80 so he handed over a couple of crisp £50 notes. Helen, having no idea that the gentleman she was serving was a world-famous footballer and the experience of accepting £50 notes being rare, spent the next two minutes holding the notes up to the light shining through the window, struggling to find the watermarks. I was cringing with embarrassment.

Square Records, Wimborne – Paul Holman

Like many shops we will always try and go the extra mile to help our customers. One day an elderly gentleman informed us he'd been trying to get a CD called *Thirty Five Not Out* by legendary jazz cornet player Digby Fairweather, but he couldn't find it anywhere. We like a challenge and promised the gentleman that we would do our utmost to track it down.

It eventually turned out that the only way we could get hold of the album was from Digby's own website. One of the sales team, Kerry, had a Paypal account which she used for buying and selling on eBay, so she offered to purchase the CD. When the package arrived, to her horror she noticed that Digby had scribbled 'To Kerry, thanks for buying the CD, hope you enjoy it, Digby Fairweather.' But to our relief the customer was so pleased we had managed to track down the CD he was happy to buy it, even with the dedication to Kerry!

* * *

An elderly lady provided us with an unusual request: she was after the new CD by Mary Whitehouse, the notorious social activist famed for her opposition to portrayals of sex and bad language in film and the media. We eventually worked out that what she was actually looking for was Amy Winehouse – talk about being poles apart!

Tangled Parrot, Carmarthen – Matt Davies

I will never forget my first day of trading; money was so short that I displayed my records and CDs in apple boxes that I'd obtained from a farm. I was delighted with my first day's takings of £60! I ploughed my money into expanding the stock but the problem was any record that didn't sell quickly soon picked up the aroma of apples from my boxes. It was quite funny to get records on the Apple label which actually smelled of the fruit!

Terry's Music, Pontypridd – Terry Rees

A gentleman visited our stall every Saturday and used to stare at us until he was served (hence his nickname, 'Mr Starey'). It didn't matter how many customers were in front of him in the queue, no matter how long he waited for his turn the request was always the same: "Elvis". We'd proceed to read out every Elvis track, with the same response – he had them all. I made it a personal challenge to find an Elvis CD that 'Mr Starey' didn't have. Whenever I do find one, it gives me great satisfaction. The downside to this is that Mr Starey always gives us a rendition of the new-to-him Elvis songs as somebody once told him he sounded like him!

One day my son, who worked with me, had his back to the counter and when he turned round 'Mr Starey' was right in front of him holding six Eagles CDs. "Who is this?" asked Mr Starey.

"The Eagles!" my son replied.

"Yes?" said 'Mr Starey'.

"Yes!" replied my son. There was silence for a while, until Mr Starey pulled out his wallet and bought the lot.

'Mr Starey' continued to come to us every week, buying the odd Elvis CD until recently I noticed him staring at me holding eight David Alexander cassettes – he bought the lot, of course.

Tesco supermarket, Liverpool – Anonymous

Even supermarkets have tales about the record-buying public. One young lady who worked at Tesco told me how she was serving an elderly gentleman and he asked if he could pay for his CDs with a cheque. "Of course!" she replied, and told him who to make the cheque out to. When he handed it over she asked him why it said Tesco 'doors'.

"That's who you told me to make the cheque out to".

"No sir," she said, trying to smother a giggle, "I said Tesco *Stores*!"

The Outback, Hereford – Madeleine Pownson

We have a sailor who often calls in before he is due to set sail, as he likes to stock up on music before he departs. One day he came in after clearly spending a bit of time in the local pub and rather sheepishly asked my assistant Caroline and I if he could ask us an embarrassing question. After a little bit of hesitation he said, "Do you stock jazz?"

We both smiled and told him there was no reason for him to be embarrassed about buying jazz – thousands of people love it and it is still very popular.

He looked at us for a few seconds before saying "Well, that wasn't the question I was going to ask!"

"What was the question then?" we enquired.

"Will either of you have sex with me?"

Caroline hastily replied. "Not on a wet Wednesday afternoon we won't!"

He scarpered out of the shop, but what made us laugh wasn't the fact that he'd asked to have sex, but that he didn't mind which one of us he was going to do it with!

The next week we both received a lovely bunch of flowers from our sailor. We were delighted and relieved that he was trying a more romantic approach – although the answer was still no!

The Record Shop, Amersham – Graeme Campbell

A famous resident of Amersham and a customer of ours was Leo Sayer. Whenever he called in he would always check his own section to see what was in stock so I felt obliged to keep his CDs up-to-date to keep my famous customer happy. In fact, I reckon there wasn't another shop in the world that had a better Leo Sayer section; it was twice as big as The Beatles and Rolling Stones' sections put together!

We enjoyed his visits but sadly his CDs didn't sell well. One day he told us he was emigrating to Australia. Much as we liked him, we couldn't wait for him to go so we could reduce the prices of his CDs in our sale and free up a lot of space in our racks.

* * *

Customer: "I've been asked to pick up a copy of the Pink Floyd album 'Bright Side Of The Sun' for a friend."

Shop: "I think your friend is winding you up!

* * *

Two elderly ladies came in and asked which André Rieu CDs and DVDs were available. I spent 20 minutes looking up titles on the computer, explaining that we could import from America and Europe. Every time I mentioned a title they would discuss it among themselves before deciding it was either too dear, they didn't like the sound of it or they already had it. Suddenly the phone rang in the back office and I excused myself, explaining that I needed to answer it and my assistant Richie would take over. I was on the call for about 10 minutes and when I returned to the counter the shop was empty. "Thank goodness those women have gone; I thought I was going to be on the computer all morning looking for stuff they were never going to buy!"

Richie started turning a shade of red and at that moment the two elderly ladies popped their heads above the counter and said, "We did buy something and we just bent down to put it in our bag, but we won't be buying anything from this shop again!"

Those Old Records, Rugeley – Chris McGranahan

A few days after I opened a man came in, looked around and said "Don't know why you bothered opening here mate, you'll never sell any records in Rugeley!". He'd obviously neglected to notice that right at that moment I was taking £350 from a customer in exchange for an original copy of a *Please Please Me* LP.

* * *

Customer: Do you buy records?"
Shop: "Yes."
Customer: "Good! I couldn't sell any of these at the car boot yesterday
            so I thought you might like to buy them?"

* * *

A customer who spent nearly three hours in the shop without speaking eventually walked to the counter with a 50p single and said "What's your best price on this mate?"

Trading Post, Stroud – Simon Vincent

One Christmas Eve we were asked if we had 'Lonely This Christmas' by Elvis Presley. I explained to the customer that it wasn't Elvis who'd sung the song, but the group Mud. The customer was adamant that he'd seen Elvis Presley with a ventriloquist's dummy singing it on *TOTP2* the night before. I reiterated that it was definitely not Elvis singing, to which he replied, "Ah yes, I think you're right – it wasn't Elvis singing, it was the dummy!"

* * *

Customer: "How much is this CD?"
Shop: "Only £8.99."
Customer: "Blimey, for that price I could buy it!" He then proceeded
            to put the CD back in the rack before leaving empty-
            handed.

JG Windows, Newcastle-upon-Tyne – Dave McGovern

Customer: "Have you got a song by a woman with love in the title? I
            heard it on the radio and would like to buy it."
Shop: "If you tell us when you heard it and what radio station it
            was on we can look up their playlist and get it for you."
Customer: "That's fantastic – the station was Radio 2 and it was about
            10 years ago."

X-Records, Bolton – Steve Meekings

X-Records has hosted many personal appearances, the most memorable of which was the time Bruce Dickinson, Iron Maiden's lead singer, played an acoustic set in the shop. Bruce was promoting his debut solo album Tattooed Millionaire by touring independent record shops and doing acoustic sets in a few each day. The event was a huge success, with the shop packed to the rafters, and after his performance Bruce was happy to sign anything the fans put in front of him. Eventually he told me he'd have to go to the next performance, but little did he know when he uttered those words that he'd be staying at X-Records for a few hours more: Bruce left the shop by the back door to return to his tour van parked in our yard only to discover that it had been clamped! I was so embarrassed, when the clampers eventually arrived to free the van I paid the fee myself.

2

Tales from HMV record shops

Have you got...?

The Phenomenal Handicap Band	(The Phenomenal Handclap Band)
Dennis Rissole	(Demis Roussos)
Frank Gillis	(Vangelis)
Shirley's Crow	(Sheryl Crow)
DJ Ango Rineheart	(Django Reinhardt)
Ernie Stubbs	(Ernest Tubb)
Rita Cool Fridge	(Rita Coolidge)
Kick Me In The Coconuts	(Kid Creole & The Coconuts)
Tommy Eros	(Tori Amos)
Raper's Delight	('Rapper's Delight', Sugarhill Gang)
No Mule You Fool	('No More The Fool', Elkie Brooks)
Sudden Leigh-on-Sea	('Suddenly I See', KT Tunstall)

HMV Brighton

One day the manager told me he'd been given two tickets to see Barry Manilow that night in Brighton but didn't really fancy going, so would I like them. Not being a fan, I made an excuse such as I was washing my hair or taking the dog for a walk and politely declined.

The manager asked each member of staff in turn but nobody wanted to take the tickets off his hands. Eventually he decided it would be best to give them to a member of the public rather than let them go to waste. He stood on the shop floor and shouted over the music that was playing. "Ladies and gentlemen, I have two free tickets here for anybody who would like to go to see Barry Manilow tonight!" Nobody said a thing. He tried again "Come on, surely somebody must want them? They're free!"

A voice piped up from behind "Doesn't anybody wish to see me?" It was Barry Manilow himself, in the shop to purchase some CDs! Unbeknown to the manager, he'd been standing behind him as he made his announcement – no wonder the customers had reacted so strangely!

HMV Dublin

In Ireland, bomb threats were a part of everyday life and it was not unusual for shops in Dublin to receive them, although they would usually turn out to be hoaxes.

I was a manager at HMV Dublin and one day took a call from what I thought was a dalek making a bomb threat; the caller was disguising his voice by speaking through a contraption that changed his vocal tone. Unfortunately I was struggling to understand what the man was saying, much to the caller's annoyance – I kept expecting him to say "Exterminate, exterminate!"

Pinned on the wall above the phone, HMV had listed fifteen questions the manager was to ask should the store receive a phone threat. I looked at the list; by the time I'd ask them all, the bomb may well have exploded. So instead I decided the first and most important question to ask was "When will the bomb go off?" After that, I reverted to the order on the list, which included the classic "Why are you doing this?" The problem for me was, because the man sounded like a dalek, I had to keep asking him to repeat his answers. Eventually the potential bomber lost patience and put the phone down. HMV staff and the rest of the shopping centre were evacuated but luckily it turned out to be a hoax and the shop was not, in fact, exterminated.

HMV Edinburgh

On my first week I was sent to the storeroom at the top of the building to get some metal racking. Before I went up the loss prevention supervisor (yes, HMV had one of those back then) told me to beware of the seagulls as they'd made a nest up there. I had to wear a hard hat and a high visibility luminous green vest for health and safety, and he armed me with a broom to fight off the seagulls in case they attacked me. I set off like a soldier going in to battle, determined to bring back the racking and see off the seagulls.

I crept up to the room and opened the door slowly, not wishing to disturb the aggressive birds. I kept the broom above my head so I could swat any attacker that swooped down. The tension was so great I could hear my heart thumping through my chest. After slowly opening the door I switched on the light. There were no seagulls there, just the racking – it had been a total wind-up, made worse by the fact that the rest of the staff had been watching me make a fool of myself on the CCTV!

HMV Hull

I was the manager of HMV Hull and while changing a display in the window, I recognised the people walking down the street as being the winners of the 1981 Eurovision Song Contest Bucks Fizz. I dashed to the stockroom, grabbed all the band's albums the shop was stuck with and went chasing after them. Once I'd caught up with them I asked if they could sign my records, explaining that I was the manager of HMV, not some dedicated fan walking around Hull with bundles of Bucks Fizz records in the hope of meeting my idols.

The band were charming but explained that they were in a hurry as they had a gig at the City Hall that evening – if I could bring the records to the show, they'd sign them after the performance. So dedicated was I back then that I boxed the records up and that evening sat through a whole performance of Bucks Fizz with the box on my lap. I have to confess I quite enjoyed the gig. True to their word, after the show the band signed the albums and the next day I put a notice in the shop window saying 'Signed Bucks Fizz Albums Available Here'. The stock sold out in a few hours.

HMV Leeds

A teenager came into the shop and asked for Ray Parker, Jr's theme tune for *Ghostbusters*. I pointed out that the single was long deleted but had a look through the racks and found the soundtrack.

The customer was delighted. As I was ringing up the sale on the till the young man explained that the record was to be played at his grandfather's funeral as he'd flown with the RAF in the war. I thought it was a bizarre choice and it was only after the young man had left the shop that I suspected he might have asked for the wrong record. Sure enough, later that day he returned to explain that he'd lightened the mood in his house as what his family had asked him to buy was the theme from *The Dambusters*, 'The Dambusters March', a famous piece of music written by British composer Eric Coates in celebration of the RAF who, with the help of bouncing bombs, had destroyed German dams in World War 2. I still think it would have been extremely funny to see his grandfather's coffin vanish behind the curtain with Ray Parker Junior asking "Who you gonna call?" and the backing singers responding with "Ghostbusters!"

* * *

Customer: "Do you have any music by Beth Oven?"
Assistant: "Do you mean Beth Orton?"
Customer: "No, it is definitely Beth Oven! I was reading about him in a magazine. He sounded good but died hundreds of years ago and I thought I would check him out."

Assistant: "Is it Beethoven?"
Customer: "That's the one!"

*   *   *

Customer: "Have you got that song about that dead bird sung by the
            guy at the piano?"

After a bit of detective work it turned out to be Elton John's tribute to HRH
Princess Diana – 'Candle In The Wind 1997'.

HMV Liverpool

One day a lady approached the counter and asked for the song 'Nuts Old
Hazelnuts'. I looked it up on the database and couldn't find any information
on a track of that name. The young lady insisted that I must know it as it was
used in an advert for chocolate. I asked if she could sing a few lines and she
burst out with: "Nuts Old Hazelnuts, Cadbury's take them and they cover
them in chocolate!" I burst out laughing, realising she meant whole hazelnuts
as opposed to old hazelnuts – it was hard to believe that Cadburys were using
old hazelnuts in their chocolate! (The song used in the advert was actually a
play on the Harry Belafonte number 'The Banana Boat Song', which people
recognise as soon as they hear the opening line "Day-O!")

*   *   *

"Do you stock the CD 'Polaroid'?" was another strange request. The staff
pointed out they had Ringo Starr's 'Photograph' and Flock of Seagulls'
'Wishing I Had A Photograph Of You', but no song called 'Polaroid'.

The lady informed us that apparently it was a classic by the band Black
Sabbath.

"Ah, I think you mean 'Paranoid'!" came the reply.

*   *   *

Customer: "Have you got the song about the arsehole man?"
Shop: "No, never heard of it."

Customer:	"You must know it, it's always on the radio!"
Shop:	"Can you sing it?'"
Customer:	"I'm Arsehole Man, da, da, da, da, da, da, I'm Arsehole Man!"
Shop:	"I think you will find the song is 'I'm A Soul Man' by Sam & Dave!"

HMV Manchester

American rock band Paramore played HMV Manchester to a massive crowd which had gathered to see them perform. The shop manager organised refreshments for the band and gave them a room on the first floor of the shop to change in. The gig was to start at 5 p.m. and a couple of minutes before that the manager asked them to come downstairs, whereupon he would announce them. He set off down and stood next to the temporary stage, waiting for the band to follow him but they didn't appear. A few minutes later a rather stressed assistant rushed over to the manager and informed him that Paramore were stuck in the lift. The shop has a lift used for transferring stock between floors and it is really only designed to hold two people plus stock – not only had the band squeezed into the lift, but their road crew had somehow crammed in as well!

The manager made his announcement to the waiting crowd. "Ladies and gentleman, I am delighted to announce that tonight we have one of the most exciting bands in the world to play for you, but for the moment they are stuck in our lift – I'll keep you updated!"

The band was truly stuck and nothing the HMV team could do would shift the lift. The manager continued to make regular announcements, only to confirm that Paramore were still stuck. Eventually he announced the bad news, that the band were still stuck, and the good news, that a lift engineer was on his way. This went down well with the crowd, which was enjoying the comical proceedings.

Eventually the engineer turned up and soon released the band. As they fell out of the lift the manager tried to lift (forgive the pun) the atmosphere by saying, "It wouldn't be the same without a Spinal Tap moment!" His humour was lost on Paramore who, as they reached the stage, seemed completely unaffected by their claustrophobic experience. In their career they will probably play hundreds of gigs but one they will never forget was that day at HMV Manchester.

* * *

Ours was a great shop for organising personal appearances. Our most impressive was when we booked one of the city's favourite sons, Morrissey. I turned up for work at 8 a.m. and there were already over a hundred people queuing outside to meet the man himself, who was due to commence signing copies of his new album, 1992's *Your Arsenal*, at 5p.m. that evening, some nine hours later.

By lunchtime crash barriers had been erected as the queue stretched along Market Street. By mid-afternoon they started letting people in and the crowd snaked through the store. When Morrissey arrived I asked him if he needed anything. He requested we play early Siouxsie & The Banshees music until it was time for him to start signing.

Later, as I walked through the crowded store I became aware of a foul smell. It was urine. Not wanting to lose their long-held places in the queue, some customers had urinated on the shop floor. Despite this unfortunate occurrence, Morrissey stayed for over three hours and the night was deemed a success.

* * *

I was a big fan of Elvis Costello, who under the pseudonym 'The Imposter' released the single 'Pills And Soap', an attack on the changes in British society brought about by Thatcherism. It was released to coincide with the run-up to the 1983 general election. I persuaded our singles buyer to order vast quantities as I was convinced it would be a smash hit. Unfortunately for Elvis and me Margaret Thatcher easily won the election, nobody was interested in buying the record, and the shop was left with a lot of stock.

One day I was told that Elvis Costello was actually in the shop browsing through the LP racks. I approached Elvis and asked him if he fancied signing a few of the singles, not mentioning of course that this was a last resort to get rid of them. Elvis obliged and I put a note up in the shop saying 'Signed Singles Available' — and what was once an overstock sold out in hours!

* * *

One day a 6 foot man dressed as a banana hopped into the shop. He bounced around our racks, still hopping on one foot while he browsed. We joked among ourselves about what he would buy; we were desperate for him to come to the counter and ask for Radiohead's 'Banana Co.', The Dickies' 'Banana Splits', Spike Jones' 'Yes! We Have No Bananas' or anything by Bananarama! Sadly it was not to be, as after 10 minutes of browsing he hopped out, waving to us all as he went.

* * *

You would think the life of a rock star would be what many people aspire to, but one person who clearly wasn't happy with his lot was Jean-Jacques Burnel, bass player with one of the finest bands to emerge from the punk era, The Stranglers, still going strong today. The band was doing a signing in HMV Manchester and before they started we offered them a cup of tea in the stockroom. Jean-Jacques was explaining to the staff how tough and tiring life on the road was. "You know, after we've finished here we have to get a flight to Paris tonight!" said Jean-Jacques.

"I know how you feel!" replied a staff member. "After I've finished here I have to get the bus back to Whalley Range!"

HMV Oldham

During my first day working for HMV I was asked by a gentleman for 'strapping young lad'. I said, "Excuse me, I can't help," I said, not knowing that Strapping Young Lad were a Canadian extreme metal band.

* * *

Customer:	"Do you have the new iPod shuttle?"
Shop:	"Apple are good but not that good – do you mean the iPod Shuffle?"
Customer:	"Ah yeah, Shuffle!"

* * *

A girl aged around seven was walking round the music department of HMV with her father and seemed baffled by the racks of CDs. "What are these Dad?" she asked.

"CDs!" he replied.

The young girl look confused before asking again "Are CDs Playstation games?"

3

Tales from record shops of the past

Have you got...?

The Loneliest Monk	(Thelonious Monk)
Barclay James Harvester	(Barclay James Harvest)
Edison Lighthouse Family	(Edison Lighthouse or The Lighthouse Family)
Andy Roo	(Andre Rieu)
Arctic Gorillaz	(Arctic Monkeys or Gorillaz)
Dee Ten	(Dio)
Zed Zed Top	(ZZ Top)
Bob Miller	(Bob Marley)
Parrot Eyes	('Paradise', Coldplay)
Streets Of Ivors	('Street Survivors', Lynyrd Skynyrd)

CE Hudson & Son, Chesterfield

One day a customer asked me "Do you have Marsha Cup?"

Although I hadn't heard of Marsha I presumed that she was a soul singer. After checking the soul section, where there was no sign of her, I looked in the 'C' of the rock and pop section but still no luck. "Where did you hear Marsha?" I asked the man.

"Sorry," he replied, "Marsha Cup is the name of the song. It is the one that goes 'I'm in love, I'm Marsha Cup!'"

"I think you'll find the lyrics are 'I'm in love, I'm all shook up' and the song is by Elvis Presley!"

* * *

Back in the early Fifties we would post our orders to London. The ordered stock was transported by steam train on Saturday mornings before being transferred by van to the shop to arrive mid-morning. I decided that it would be best to pick up the stock from the railway station when the steam train arrived at 4.30 a.m. I'd take a taxi, as the shop didn't have a van and I didn't own a car; the reason I did this was that so we could have the stock on the shelf by opening time.

In those days every record had to be checked before going on display, as shops suffered a high percentage of breakages – 78s were very brittle and needed to be packed carefully. This would seem obvious but the record companies delivered their product in tea chests packed with straw; the straw came in handy for the local horses but was useless at protecting records! I recall one Christmas when the delivery was so big it hardly fitted in the taxi! The driver was reluctant to set off with so much weight on board but I promised him a big tip if he was prepared to risk it. The tip was much needed by the end of the journey, as each time we went over a bump one of the taxi's wheel hubs flew off.

* * *

One gig that had an impact on the town and our shop was the night Engelbert Humperdinck played the Regal Theatre and one of the support acts was Jimi

Hendrix. The next day the gig was the talk of the town. Some who attended thought the wild guitarist they had witnessed had ruined the show while many came in the next day to buy this new and exciting artist's record. The agent who put them on the same bill deserved sacking, as they went together like bananas and gravy!

* * *

Dress Circle, London

John Barrowman did a personal appearance in the shop and was asked to sign a fan's arm so they could tattoo over his signature. He agreed, on one condition: that the fan would sign a contract absolving him of any blame if the tattoo went septic or the fan had to have his arm amputated.

Mike Lloyd Music, Hanley

On my first day, I was shocked to find that every other member of staff disappeared just as a curious old chap with a long white beard arrived at the counter. This was my first encounter with the notorious customer known as Sir Alan Maddock.

Sir Alan would come into the store every day at the same time and ask whether his order had come in (for the *Flying Down To Rio* LP – which, of course, was impossible to order having long been deleted). While the staff would attempt to get him to understand that we wouldn't be able to get it for him, eventually they would give up and say that there was nothing in on that day for him so he should try again at a later date!

Sir Alan would always tell us a tale, such as he was about to go on a date with Grace Kelly, or how Boris Karloff was his uncle. Another classic I recall was the time he told me he was once hung, but didn't die because his legs were so long they touched the floor. He bought a calendar of George Clooney because he thought George was the 'Earl of Stafford', while he once forgot how to walk between counter and door... I could go on...!

Tales from Music Zone

Customer: Do you have any 'Larry and Hardly' DVDs? (Laurel and Hardy)

* * *

Customer: "Hi, I'm after a song I've just heard on the radio... "
Shop: "No problem, do you know what it's called?"
Customer: "Oh... erm... no, I didn't catch the name of it."
Shop: "Do you know who it's by?"
Customer: "No... I missed what the DJ bloke said. I think it's in the charts."
Shop: "Hmm, Ok... do you know any of the lyrics? Can you sing a bit of it?"
Customer: "Eeeee! I'm not singing it to you!" (awkward pause) "I think a man sings it... "

* * *

Customer: "Do you have a CD by Jamie MacKay please?"
Shop: (After much thought) "Is it Jamiroquai you're looking for?"
Customer: "Oh no, it's definitely Jamie Mackay!"

We played a Jamiroquai album and asked if this was what he was after.

Customer: "Yes that's Jamie!"

* * *

Customer: "Have you got that CD by Leslie Miserables?" (The musical and now film *Les Miserables...*)

* * *

While I was managing the Oldham store, we had a regular customer who walked in, picked up a copy of each of the Top 10 CDs and took them to the counter. He then told me he already had them and asked for a full refund. I pointed out that some had only been released on that day, none of them had discs in and I'd just watched him take them off the shelf! The first time it happened I banned him, but he returned the following week and did the same, then the next week and the one after that. This happened for about two months and it actually became a joke. Then, one week he bought about 40 CDs and never came back... strange character indeed!

* * *

Like many shops, the staff at Music Zone gave some of their customers nicknames. Luckily they saved the list – here are some of the more bizarre characters:

Andy and Lou: A man and a woman named after the characters in Matt Lucas and David Walliams' television sketch comedy show *Little Britain.* 'Andy and Lou' only had one wheelchair between them and took it in turns to wheel each other around in it. They did spend a ridiculous amount of money in the store though, and the man was always polite. The lady never spoke, only ever staring vacantly into the middle distance.

Crazy Singing Chinese Lady: Made famous for her love of humming songs and expecting us to figure them out.

Hagrid: An unkempt man with body odour and a long beard. One day he came to the counter carrying a cooked chicken, which he was eating – no wrapping, just stuffing the meat into his mouth.

Another time Hagrid bought a few CDs and later left his Music Zone bag with the CDs he had purchased on a bench. Some kids brought them into the store and exchanged them for something else. Later that day he returned to say he'd lost his CDs and he bought back the exact copies he'd purchased earlier! I felt pretty harsh selling him the same CDs twice but I hadn't realised they were his when the kids brought them in.

Lass Vegas: A rather large lady who not only looked like the comedian Johnny Vegas but sounded like him, too.

"When is the January sale starting?" she would bellow.

Our answer was always the same: "January!"

Mr Compton: He asked for our names and then called us different ones. He came in every Tuesday to give us newspaper clippings of the articles he'd found interesting.

Smug Git: One day 'Smug Git' bought an Oasis CD, then 20 minutes later he returned with a grin, slid the CD across the counter and said, "It's scratched, I want my money back! I examined the CD and there wasn't a mark on it, which is what I told him. "Well," he said, "I've seen it cheaper across the road – can I have a refund?" I said no. Not only was he changing his story quicker than Cher changes costumes/faces, but he'd been rude to me and my staff. "Are you telling me that you'd rather lose my valuable custom than give me £6?"

I rested both hands on the counter, looked him straight in the eye and said "Yes!"

Immediately security escorted off the premises. As he walked out the door, he stopped, turned and pointed at me (his hand sideways, like the way Samuel L. Jackson points his gun in the movie *Pulp Fiction*) and said "You never went to business school, did you motherf**ker?"

Sweaty Glasses Man: This guy used to spend forever selecting his discs. The decision-making must have stressed him out because by the time he reached the counter he would be leaking onto the work surfaces! He would always pay with a cheque, which also ended up covered in his dripping sweat.

The Cat Women: A mother and daughter who smelled like a cross between a cat's litter tray that hadn't been emptied for years and wet dog hair. Every time they came in we all had to cover our noses and as soon as they left, the staff had to take it in turns to spray the shop with air freshener.

The Price-changing Family: They would change the price labels on CDs then bring them to the counter and think we wouldn't notice!

The Wanderer: He would come in, walk up the left side of the shop then down the right side without stopping, the whole time looking at the floor. He'd then go into Woolworth and do the same! He never spoke except once to ask for a *Chariots Of Fire* DVD.

Wannabe Gangster Kid: He spoke with a fake American accent and threatened to "pop a cap in yo' ass" if the CD he wanted had sold out when he came to get it on a Monday.

Wheels: This guy had a purple beard and was in a wheelchair. He also wore a crash helmet. I asked him why he wore his crash helmet all the time and he replied "I hurt my head once leaning forward to pick up the remote control for the TV."

One Stop, London

A man came to the counter and asked for 'Middle of the Record'.

"Don't you mean 'Middle of the Road'?" I asked. (Middle of the Road was a Scottish group who'd won a TV talent programme called *Opportunity Knocks*. They released three singles in 1971, selling an incredible 10 million copies worldwide).

"No" said the man, "I mean the middle of a record!"

I was flummoxed and thought I was dealing with a nutcase! How could somebody walk into a record shop with 20,000 plus titles in stock and not want a record but just the middle of one? It was at this point that another staff

member pointed out that we *did* in fact stock middles and they were under the counter. In the Seventies a lot of the 7″ singles imported from abroad arrived in the UK with the centre punched out so the singles would fit into jukeboxes – apparently our customer needed his middles back so he could play the singles on his record player!

* * *

Our best customer was a young singer-songwriter who was, and still is, a music fanatic – he bought more records than any other customer. I really enjoyed dealing with him and each week would put records aside that I felt he would like. Such was his love of the place that when things got busy, he happily helped serve behind the counter. It was great to see the look on the face of the customers when they recognised the assistant serving them was none other than Elton John!

Tales from Our Price

Customer: "I'm looking for Tom Waits."
New staff member: "Sorry, he doesn't work here."

* * *

An American teenager came in and asked me "Have you got that song called Fruity Bacon?" I explained I hadn't heard of it so he volunteered to sing it.

"Y'know, it goes 'We're so fruity, oh so fruity, yeah – we're bacon!' After I stifled my laughter I suggested it was 'Pretty Vacant' by the Sex Pistols!

* * *

One day a guy joined the back of a 30-minute queue in the Brent Cross branch of Our Price. It was a very busy Saturday and he was carrying his full stack system (turntable, cassette player, speakers – the lot!) When he finally got to the counter, looking exhausted and sweating profusely, he managed to breathlessly squeak "Do you have a stylus for this mate?" Poor chap – Our Price didn't even sell them!

* * *

Customer:	"Have you got 'Pale Blue Eyes'?"
Shop:	"I think they are more green than blue."
Customer:	"No, it's a song by the Velvet Underground!"

*   *   *

Customer:	"I'm after a song I heard in the Rose & Crown pub the other night, it was Beat 2."
Shop:	"Is Beat 2 the artist or the song?"
Customer:	"No, it is B2 – the number on the jukebox!"

*   *   *

Customer:	"I'd like my money back on these CDs please."
Shop:	"Why's that sir?"
Customer:	"I don't like them!"
Shop:	"Sorry sir, company policy is we can only exchange faulty goods."
Customer:	"What kind of store are you? If you brought anything back to my shop that you didn't like we'd instantly refund your money."
Shop:	"Where do you work sir?"
Customer:	"Marks & Spencer."
Shop:	"Yes, but you can't play jumpers, can you?"

*   *   *

I was working at Waterloo station branch, a very busy store as you can imagine, trading over 15 hours' a day, 7 days' a week. The store was frequented by all types of people, particularly the homeless, who would come in for the heat after their nights camped under Waterloo Bridge. One elderly chap visited us the same time every day, and pretended to be interested in our range, pointing and flicking through the CDs so as to be seen as a genuine customer. We felt sorry for his situation and allowed him to remain in the store even though his occasional manic laughter caused a few turned heads.

One day he was particularly spaced-out and we noticed a few people standing outside the store looking in – in no time, a crowd began to gather. Being in a station we didn't think much of it, until we noticed an odd shape appearing above the racking at the front of the store. I was asked to go and investigate and was shocked to see what can only be described as a miniature, scale-copy of Stonehenge, erected from a collection of CDs — cases open, carefully placed on top of each other, well over a metre tall! I didn't really know what to do, as the crowd seemed rather pleased with his efforts and as I dismantled his work of art I received boos from his adoring fans!

* * *

At the height of Spice Girls fever, on Christmas Eve myself and four other lads in the store decided to dress as the 'Girl Power five' themselves (I was Posh as I had long dark hair back then). Towards the end of my shift the boss instructed me to change the window posters. She had a wry smirk on her face but I thought nothing of it. While in the window I was bending over and reaching to get the sale posters up and when I turned around I had an audience of ladies staring, giggling and pointing at me; I'd forgotten about my rather short dress and not realised I'd been exposing my backside to the passing shoppers. I'd like to think I increased the shop's sales that day...

* * *

One customer we christened 'Mr Bean' (there was a great resemblance) would go out of his way to ask questions that either could not be answered or to which he knew the answer already. He asked week after week about a Kylie import that was never going to come into Our Price and was given that very answer for what must have been years. Once, after the release of Spice Girl Mel B's solo album, he brought a copy over to me rather excitedly, pointing out in the lyric book that she used the word 'bastard' in track seven, yet there was no parental advisory sticker on the box. I found one and stuck it on and he still didn't buy the bloody thing! Another time he brought a DVD to the counter pointing out the 18 certificate on the front, the back and the spine, but it was missing from the disc. I thought he was going to explode with joy at his discovery. I withdrew it from sale.

* * *

A woman came into the Liverpool store and asked for 'Rock Around The Clock' by Bill Shankly.

Although Liverpool football fans claimed he could walk on water, even the great man himself can't be credited with being the father of rock'n'roll! The assistant suggested the woman was probably after Bill Haley's version…

* * *

Customer: "Do you remember the song 'Toast'?"
Shop: "Yes, it was a minor hit sung by Paul Young when he was in a group called The Streetband. We don't have it in stock but I'll see if I can order it."
Customer: "Oh, I don't want it – I just think it would be funny if The Jam, Marmalade or Bread did a cover version!"

* * *

Customer: "Could you tell me where The Doors are please?"
Shop assistant: "Yes they're at the front of the shop – that's how you got in!"

* * *

An old lady approached the counter asking for a refund; she'd bought a CD by the band Jesus & Mary Chain, thinking it was going to be religious music!

* * *

Customer: "Do you have the record that people dance to like this?"
            (He jumped to one side, arms by his sides, then bounced between the CD racks).

I looked at him, dumbfounded, before calling over the manager for a second opinion, although I admit I just wanted to see the customer jumping around the shop again! The manager then proceeded to call the assistant manager just so we could witness the now exhausted customer demonstrate his shaking one more time. We never did work out which song the twinkle-toed customer was after!

Purple Haze, Plymouth

We nicknamed our favourite customer 'Kanu Gettit' as his opening line was always "Can you get it?" Sadly he would often burst into tears if we were unsuccessful in tracking down the records he was after.

Roots, Newcastle-upon-Tyne

Customer: "I'm after this record but I don't know who sings it or what it's called… it sounded like Bob Dylan singing on an old radio, but it wasn't Bob!"

In 1998, the shop was finally hooked up to the Internet. I was really excited by this and one day a girl I liked came in so I tried to impress her with this new concept. "Look!" I said to her, "if I put The Waterboys (her favourite band) in here, press enter, you get… oh, gay Japanese porn… "

Rotate Records, Brighouse

Gary Numan fans were fanatical about their idol and would turn up at 9.01 a.m. on a Monday morning (the day of a new release) and buy every different format of the same new Gary Numan track. Sometimes they walked out with three or four copies of the same record – God knows what they did with them! Buying more than one copy sends that particular single rocketing up the charts during week one; after that it's all over. No one else buys it and on week two you may as well put everything left over in the 20p dump bin – no self-respecting Gary Numan fan ever bought a single on week two.

A sales rep from one of the promotion companies came in each week with his "Portfolio of Dreams", which is what he called his folder containing all the singles he was promoting and selling that week (it was just a plastic folder with a copy of a single in each pocket). He wasn't a pushy rep and I looked forward to him coming round; he was a good laugh! He'd just dump his folder on the counter and asked me to "peruse through the crap" then tell him what I wanted. "You might want to listen to that one," he would say, "people seem to be interested in that one, but don't bother sticking it on unless you wish to clear the shop – it's absolute rubbish!" At the end of the folder, after the albums and cassettes, there were also carpets and curtain fabrics – nothing to do with the promotions company he was working for, of course – he just added them himself for a little bit of extra cash!

* * *

My worst day was when I bought 50 units of the new TV-advertised *Greatest Hits* album by Gary Glitter, just a matter of days before he took his computer to be fixed at PC World...

* * *

A mature lady came in holding a piece of paper and asked for an enema for her son, not realising it was pronounced 'Eminem'...

* * *

I employed some great people but I had to 'let go' one young girl because she had absolutely no idea what she was doing and had no interest in any music outside of the Top 5. She filed things in the wrong places and couldn't tell the difference between an LP and a 12″ single. I realised that I had made the right decision when someone found the Emerson, Lake & Palmer album *Brain Salad Surgery* bagged up and filed away under Artist: Brian Salad, Title: Surgery.

Rounder Records, Brighton

We make an effort to review all the vinyl we sell and put the reviews on a white sticker, which we then display on the album. This is not unique in independent record shops but our reviews in Rounder are extremely truthful and if we don't like an album, we say so in the review. One album that felt the wrath of a scathing review was by an artist called Kris Needs. We described his album as boring, with vocals by a rather broad sounding European woman. We never expected to sell it but to our surprise a couple brought it to the counter. Instead of purchasing it the man told me that he disagreed with the review. "Why's that?" I asked.

"I'm Kris Needs!" the man replied, "And I would like to introduce you to the rather broad sounding European woman!" he said, pointing out the lady who was standing next to him. I turned a bright shade of crimson but offered Kris the opportunity to write his own review, so the album was returned to the racks with two reviews attached to it. I remember that he took it all in good humour.

* * *

A man walked in and said that he'd heard a "bangin' tune" and did we have it in stock? The only problem was he couldn't remember the artist or the title. He was asked if he could describe it.

"Yes, it went duh, duh, duh, duh, then it made some squeaky noises then duh, duh, again for ages."

"Sorry mate," the assistant said, "we've sold out!"

* * *

One of the most famous dance record labels is Defected. It received notable success with the 2001 number one single from Roger Sanchez called 'Another Chance'. Unsurprisingly, the label name did give us some problems; one lady came back and demanded a refund as the record she had purchased was defected. I tried to explain that the label was 'Defected' and that was why it was written all over the record. The lady wasn't listening to me and admonished me for selling faulty goods, saying if she didn't get a refund her next call was to Trading Standards. I didn't have the heart to argue further and gave her a refund just to shut her up.

The Music Box, Wallingford

Sony Records invited me to a showcase evening held in a huge warehouse in London. These events were hosted by record companies to highlight new bands and the lucky guests tended to be journalists and record shop owners, the people whose help would be needed to champion these new artists. The evening usually revolved around three acts recently signed to the label, each of whom would play a few numbers then mingle with the specially invited guests. There was normally a free bar and fabulous food, and guests would receive a goody bag containing advanced copies of forthcoming releases from the performing bands. This particular night I thought that, as a treat, I would invite my younger brother to the event. He was thrilled but I laid down some ground rules, telling him it was very important that if anybody asked he should say he worked at The Music Box and if anybody from the record company enquired about what he thought of any of the bands he should say that they were brilliant.

My brother and I arrived at the warehouse and helped ourselves to the free beer. We were soon joined by many of the Sony Music executives and they all chatted about life in retail. My brother kept a low profile, since most of the conversation went over his head. By now there were eight people standing in a circle talking when a man approached: "Hey folks, great news! The sofas have arrived!"

Seizing the chance to join in on the conversation my brother piped up, "Fantastic! I think their album is brilliant and I'm looking forward to seeing them play live!"

His comments were met with a stony silence before an executive from Sony said, "The sofas are for us all to sit on – the delivery driver is late and that's why we're all standing up!" Needless to say I didn't take my brother to an industry event again!

Tower Records, New York

In 1985, I was the import buyer for the biggest record shop in the world, Tower Records in New York. I over-ordered the imported Smiths' album *Hatful Of Hollow* as it didn't appear to have a release date in the USA. In only a few brief days, several hundred of them vanished like hotcakes as I'd placed them without prior approval among the new releases that were piled high to the right as one walked into the store. I was immensely proud to have gotten away with this guerrilla act and some days after I discovered that the sales of that record from our store were deemed to represent something like 17 per cent of sales nationwide in numerous charts. Thus, I had inadvertently hyped The Smiths into the American charts (I have yet to receive a call from Morrissey inviting me for a drink!)

Valhalla Records, Kilmarnock

Customer: "I heard a song on the radio a few weeks back sung by Elvis Presley and would like to buy it on CD. The only thing is I don't want the Elvis version, I want the original!"

Shop: "Do you know the song?"

Customer: "No."

Shop: "Who sung the original?"

Customer: "Don't know."

Shop: "Do you have any other clues?"

Customer: "No!"

Then followed a 20-second pause before the customer said "Are you trying to say that you won't be able to get it then?"

Tales from Virgin Megastore

The opening of the Virgin store in Middlesbrough was supported by a poster campaign with a picture of a little old lady holding a 'granny barrow' (one of those wheeled shopping bags) and sporting a T-shirt stating 'The Only Virgin in the Boro'. This was not long after Middlesbrough had been pronounced the teenage pregnancy capital of Europe. One of the local churches, in protest at our shocking campaign, sent 12 virgins to stand outside the store and conduct some kind of candlelit vigil. They took a lot of stick from blokes passing by!

*   *   *

I was an area manager at Virgin and was sent to sort out a new Manchester shop. The first problem I encountered was that the shop had no security. After an argument with a Virgin employee, the team fitting the shop's alarm left the site; the shop had tens of thousands of pounds worth of stock and nothing to protect it! I called Head Office for advice and they asked if I could sort out a temporary solution while they tried to resolve the dispute with the alarm company. I went off into Manchester City Centre to see what I could find and came back with a mechanical guard dog. When everybody had left the store at the end of the evening I unpacked the dog and set it up – it looked like K-9 (canine) the mechanical dog, Dr Who's faithful companion back in the Seventies TV series. When I plugged it in near the entrance, the dog's eyes sent out a laser beam – if anyone walked through the beam the dog would bark! Luckily for me (and the shop) the alarm was fitted a few days later.

What Records, Nuneaton

Customer: "Have you got that song The Farmer? I don't know who sings it but it's definitely called The Farmer, it's in the charts."

I looked through the whole Top 75 – there was no reference to any farmer whatsoever so I asked if it was by The Farmer's Boys.

Customer: "No, the song is called The Farmer... I'll sing it!" she offered. "*The farmer, a licky boom boom down, the farmer!*" I realised she was singing 'Informer', the 1992 hit by Canadian reggae band Snow!

* * *

'Pet Shop Boy' was one of my favourite customers. He had a job loading lorries on the nightshift at the local industrial estate and after he'd finish his shift each day he'd come down to the shop, as he didn't want to miss a thing. In fact, most of our customers thought he worked for us!

I called him 'Pet Shop Boy' because when I first met him he was crazy for the electronic duo and bought everything they released in every format. 'Pet Shop Boy' became part of the furniture. Needless to say my boss hated him, even tried to ban him from the shop on several occasions, but I just wouldn't have it – he was a local face, people liked him, I liked him, and he brought custom into the shop.

On the quiet days when I worked alone he'd keep me company and on days when we had hired help in (usually our Saturday girl in need of extra hours) we'd have a game of football in the park or go over to the pub. One day 'Pet Shop Boy' approached the counter, brandishing two guns.

"What are you doing with those?" I asked. "Are you looking to do a robbery?"

"No, don't worry – they're not real, they're cap guns. Fancy a game?' he asked.

"A game of what?" I replied.

"Cowboys and Indians!"

I don't know what possessed me to agree to this, maybe I wanted to relive my childhood as it was over 20 years since I'd last played a game of Cowboys and Indians, but I agreed to take part in this madness. I asked my assistant to mind the shop as I was just nipping out the back.

"To do what?" she asked.

"Just off for a game of Cowboys and Indians!" was my embarrassing reply.

In fact, me and 'Pet Shop Boy' soon entered into a fully fledged battle on the car park, shooting each other with the cap guns and locked in warfare when my boss pulled up in his car, only to see me quickly dive under the wheel of a Ford Escort in a vain attempt to hide. I sheepishly had to come out, surrender my toy weapon and take the rap for having an imaginary gunfight instead of attending to the shop.

That would have been the first of many written warnings (by 1996 I think I could have decorated my house with them).

Tales from Zavvi

"Do you have A Chocolate Orange? It's a Stanley Kubrick film…"

I was impressed they actually knew it was Stanley Kubrick who made the film they were after, even though they had the easy part wrong!

* * *

We noticed people sniggering while looking through our CD racks so went to investigate. We'd recently asked a new member of staff to make header boards and it didn't take me long to find the culprit: 'KATE'S BUSH'.

* * *

Customer: "I'm after the new CD by Snowplay." (Perhaps a new supergroup featuring members of both Snow Patrol and Coldplay?)

*   *   *

Customer: "You know the song 'Is This The Way To Amarillo'?"
Shop: "Yes, by Tony Christie."
Customer: "Where is it?"
Shop: "All our CDs are filed in alphabetical order so you will find it in the C section, but if you follow me I'll show you."
Customer: "No, it's OK, I don't want to buy it, I just wondered where Amarillo is!"

One of our regular customers was someone we called 'Minority Report Man' (or 'MRM' for short). He was often in store and caused staff to run for safety when spotted – he would pull his shopping trolley around, harassing staff and customers about aliens and alien abduction, letting us know his views on the topic. He got his nickname after one day pointing at a copy of *Minority Report* on DVD and saying to our assistant manager "I was in that film!"

The AM declared "What, *Minority Report?*"

MRM: "Yeah!"

AM: "*Minority Report*, with Tom Cruise?"

MRM: "Who's Tom Cruise?"

*   *   *

Customer:	"Do you know Jason Orange?"
Shop:	"Yes, he's in Take That."
Customer:	"Brilliant, I want to get in touch with him – can you give me his address please?"
Shop:	"I know who he is but I'm not a friend or anything… "
Customer:	"What about the rest of Take That – do you have their addresses?"
Shop:	"No… Try contacting their management."
Customer:	"Do you have the managements' address?"
Shop:	"No, sorry!"
Customer:	"I like Boyzone as well – I don't suppose you have their contact details do you?"
Shop:	"Correct!"
Customer:	"This is all rather disappointing!"

4

Tales from classical record shops

Scandinavian gentleman:	Do you sell whores?
Shop:	"I'm sorry sir, but we don't."
Scandinavian gentleman:	"I thought Oxford was famous for its whores."
Shop:	"Sir, will you please leave the shop?"
Scandinavian gentleman:	"You don't understand – it is boy whores I am looking for."
Shop:	"Sir, if you don't leave we will call the police."

As the gentleman turned around he noticed a CD and plonked it on the counter. "This is what I'm after," he said.

Shop: "Sir, the word is 'choirs' and if you go around asking for 'whores' you will get yourself into a lot of trouble!"

*   *   *

Customer: "Have you got a CD by Dinu Lipatti? The chap on the radio said he was only 33 when he passed away and he died on TV."

Shop: "He was 33 when he died – of TB."

*   *   *

Customer: "When it says 'Piano, four hands' does that mean I need two people?"

*   *   *

Customer: "Who Wrote the Fauré Requiem?"

Shop: "Fauré!"

*   *   *

Customer: "I want a CD of choirs but no choral music please!"

*   *   *

Customer: "Do you sell light bulbs?"

Shop: "I'm sorry sir, this is a classical CD shop."

Customer: "Oh well, do you have a 25 watt screw fitting?"

Shop: "I'm sorry sir, but this is still a classical CD shop."

*   *   *

Customer: "Can I buy Carmina Burana? Do you know who wrote it?"

Shop: "Carl Orff."

Customer: "Is his first name Boris?"

*   *   *

Customer: "I'm studying music and have this book which talks about G Major.

Do you have any CDs with G Major on so I can hear what it sounds like?"

* * *

Customer: "Do you have 'The Ascent Of The Lark' by Robert Vaughan?" ('The Lark Ascending' was composed by Ralph Vaughan Williams, while Robert Vaughan was the American actor best known for his role in *The Man From Uncle*).

* * *

Customer: "I'm looking for Tchaikovsky but can't find him in the C section!"

* * *

Customer: "I'm a teacher and I'm doing an assembly about hands, so I thought I'd buy some music by Handel. I thought the 'Arrival Of The Queen Of Sheba' would be a good choice as I would be able to bring in some Sheba cat food."

* * *

A lady came in with a scrap of paper with 'Donkey Oaty' scribbled on it: "Do you have this?" she asked. It took me at least five minutes to work out she was looking for the Richard Strauss piece *Don Quixote*.

* * *

Customer: "I heard this piece on the radio a while back... "
Shop: "Ah right, do you remember roughly when it was? I can look it up on the Radio 3 website"
Customer: "Yes, of course, it was when I was collecting the dog from the vet after his operation!"

* * *

Customer: "Do you have the Carry On Fidelio DVD?"

Shop: "We don't stock anything connected to Sid James, Hattie Jacques and Co."

Customer: "You don't have any Carry On operas at all? I find that incredible!"

It transpired that the man was in fact looking for Karajan conducting Fidelio.

Customer: "Hello, I'm in a hurry and I want a recording of a new piece that's receiving its world premiere at the Proms next week."

*   *   *

Customer: "I'm after an opera called Twist Of The Nut?"

Shop: "I think you'll find it's called *The Turn Of The Screw* by Benjamin Britten."

*   *   *

Customer: Have you got 'Songs of the Algarve' by Bailero?
Shop: I think you mean the song 'Baïlèro', of the *Songs From The Auvergne*, sir."

*　*　*

Customer: "I'm looking for Beethoven Piano Sonatas."
Shop: "A recording, or the sheet music?"
Customer: (As if confronted with the most impenetrable specialist jargon) "I'm sorry, that means absolutely nothing to me – what's the difference?"

*　*　*

Customer: "Do you have a CD of balalaika music from *Captain Corelli's Mandolin*?"
Shop: "We have the music but it's played on a mandolin."
Customer: "No, it is definitely played on the balalaika!"

*　*　*

Customer: "What's the difference between a four-hole and a five-hole ocarina?" (An ocarina is a wind instrument traditionally made of ceramic, with four to twelve finger holes and a mouthpiece).

*　*　*

Customer: "I heard this lovely piece of music on the radio by a chap called Haydn. Do you have it in stock?"
Shop: "Do you have any more information?"
Customer: "I thought you might say that so I wrote it down. It's called 'Symphony'."

*　*　*

Customer: "Do you have a DVD of the Greek film 'Ulysses is Gay' please?"

Shop: "I think you will find it's called *Ulysses' Gaze*!"

*   *   *

Customer: "Did Chopin only write the one *First Piano Concerto*?"

5

Tales from record company sales representatives

Have you got...?

Rubber Plant	(Robert Plant)
Insipid Carpets	(Inspiral Carpets)
Seasick Dick	(Seasick Steve)
Eric & The Dominoes	(Derek & The Dominoes)
The Shakespeare Sisters	(Shakespeare's Sister)
Linesman For The County	('Wichita Lineman', Glen Campbell, which contains the line "I am a lineman for the county")
The song about the woman jogging to the shops	('Running Up That Hill', Kate Bush)

Ian Grenfell, former sales rep for A&M, now manager to Mick Hucknall

In the early Eighties I worked with A&M as a rep for Birmingham and the Midlands. At the end of my first week I heard that one of the other reps was leaving and I was invited to join all the other record company reps in going for a leaving drink with him. They mentioned we'd be going to a club and I presumed it would be to see a band. Later we arrived at the spot, a club called The Time and The Place, in Digbeth. I surveyed the posters on the wall and soon came to the conclusion there wouldn't be a band playing, unless they were called 'Sexy Strippers Tonight' or 'Entrance only £2, includes chips, peas and faggots'! We all trooped in and someone bought me a drink. A couple of women walked past in scruffy coats carrying bags of shopping, and one of the reps informed me that they were the strippers. When the show finished I couldn't wait to get home but all the other reps were going back to one of the strippers' flat to carry on the party. As the youngest there I felt I couldn't not go. I recall sitting on the sofa nursing a drink while a Dansette record player blasted out the only two records the strippers seemed to own, Rod Stewart's 'Passion' and 'Use It Up Wear it Out' by Odyssey. To this day I have never forgotten those records, which I had to suffer while the stripper entertained the other reps. If that was a typical music industry party I decided I had joined the wrong profession. Luckily I never attended an event like that again.

A Sony rep (anonymous)

Several years ago the Sony rep for the North West organised a personal appearance for Tom Jones in HMV Liverpool. Tom attracted a huge crowd of fans, although one enthusiastic lady decided she wanted him to sign something other than his new record. "Hey Tom sign these!" she called. With that she undid her top and revealed a huge pair of boobs, which she plonked on the counter. Tom was happy to oblige but security took a dim view and ushered her away. "Get your hands off me!" she screamed as the security guard tried to remove her from the shop. As he let go the lady leaned back and thrust her head into the security guard's face knocking him to the ground. Tom had a big hit with the song 'Kiss' but the security guard will never forget the day he was on the receiving end of what is known as a 'Liverpool Kiss'.

*   *   *

On an earlier occasion, the same rep had security problems in the city. Reps faced a daily dilemma: their cars were filled with valuable CDs and records – they often carried a 1,000 units plus – making them a target for opportunist thieves. This rep had already had his car broken into twice while he was visiting record shops, and both times his entire stock had been stolen. His bosses were far from happy and he was warned he'd be in big trouble if it happened again, so next time he decided to take his family dog out with him to guard the car.

After being at a meeting with HMV he returned to his vehicle only to find to his horror that his car had been broken into again. This time, not only had they nicked the stock but they'd stolen his dog as well. Sadly both the stock and dog were never seen again.

*   *   *

Sony had some great promotions to help propel their records up the chart. One that I regret was for a single called 'We Need Protection', released in 1985 by the band Picnic in the White House. Sony had the idea to provide shops with hundreds of Picnic chocolate bars to raise awareness of the record. I was personally supplied with a huge stash of them to give away. The temptation of hundreds of boxes of chocolate bars next me while I drove around the country proved too much – for the next few weeks I found myself munching on them throughout my journeys. I ate so many that it put me off Picnics for life and my waistline really suffered while promoting that particular band.

*   *   *

Sony launched a competition for the sales team and the winner would win a trip to New York. They were releasing a single by Cyndi Lauper called 'Change Of Heart' and to promote the record they had produced some plastic puzzles to give away to the shops. The puzzle consisted of small metal balls that fitted into a plastic heart which floated on water. The first rep to post back the completed puzzle to Sony Head Office would win the prize trip to the Big Apple.

However, the problem (which was obviously a set-up) was that the slightest bit of movement would result in the balls falling out of the puzzle! I was convinced I could solve it and like some sort of mad professor I started zapping completed puzzles in my microwave. No matter how many minutes I left the puzzle in the microwave the heart in the middle would melt. I came up with another strategy of freezing the completed puzzle. The problem with this theory was that by the time the puzzle reached the Sony Head Office in London the ice would have melted. My mum came up with a solution – why not freeze the puzzle then ram it inside a frozen chicken and then post it? I bought a chicken and rammed the puzzle as far in as it would go, then put it in the freezer. The next day I sent it by the 5.30 p.m. post, certain that it would arrive first thing the following day.

Next morning I phoned my boss at Head Office and asked him to be there when Cyndi Lauper's product manager opened the parcel addressed to him. He reached inside the chicken with some trepidation and slowly pulled out the frozen puzzle. A loud cheer went around the office when the staff became aware that all the balls were in place and I had solved the game! One of the staff took photos, which appeared in the next edition of *Music Week*.

It turned out that the trip wasn't to the Big Apple, New York City, but to a restaurant of the same name in Manchester. I wasn't too bothered, as I suspected there might be a catch – anyway, it was good to outsmart the smart arse who came up with the incentive and it gave everybody in the company a good laugh.

Del Querns, former rep for Full Force, now co-owner of Music's Not Dead record shop in Bexhill-on-Sea

I got a job with Full Force, an independent promotions company working on behalf of various record companies, with the purpose of making sure shops were stocking and displaying the records we were promoting. The company would earn money depending on the chart positions of the records; to achieve a higher position we'd often give away the records to help them on their way, since a record shop's staff is going to make more of an effort to sell a CD single for £2.99 that has cost them nothing as it's all profit. Therefore, they'd usually display these particular discs on the counter. We also used to give away gifts such as T-shirts, jackets, hampers, or in one case tracksuits, anything to promote the record. Once a record had entered the chart it was no longer given away free and the shop would purchase our stock. I loved the work and a few months later I was promoted to the job of sales manager in charge of 13 other reps.

The job also involved me meeting potential customers and persuading them to employ Full Force. It was at one of these meetings I become an unlikely and somewhat notorious TV star following a sting by investigative journalist Roger Cook and his programme *The Cook Report*, a show that regularly attracted over 8 million viewers. That particular programme revealed how record companies were hyping singles into the charts. I was contacted by a person called Barry who said he had a fabulous new act that he was looking to break into the charts, so could he arrange a meeting. I invited him to meet me at the Full Force office but Barry suggested we meet at a local pub instead. What I didn't realise was that the TV production company would be there, secretly filming the meeting…

To my surprise the great new artist turned out to be Debbie Currie, the daughter of Tory MP Edwina Currie (what I didn't know was that Debbie was also working as a trainee journalist with Central TV). The song she'd recorded was a cover version of the 1973 number three hit by Limmie & The Family Cooking, 'You Can Do Magic'. I listened to the record and thought it was awful so in my mind I didn't think the daughter of a Tory MP had any chance of making the charts no matter the methods used to promote her. Barry told me that one of the most famous producers in the country, Mike Stock – who as part of the producing and songwriting team of Stock, Aitken and Waterman had been involved in over a hundred UK top 40 hits with artists such as Kylie Minogue, Rick Astley and Dead or Alive – was the record's producer. So, despite my left-wing politics and the fact that I was certain the record would be a turkey, business is business, so I agreed to take on the job of promoting the record.

Over the next couple of weeks I'd meet Barry in the pub for regular meetings and he'd probe me on how best to get the record up the charts, me not realising I was being filmed the whole time. The record was released on May 19, 1997, and *The Cook Report* went into overdrive promoting

Debbie. They lined up more than 40 press interviews and Debbie, who could genuinely sing, toured the UK's nightclubs doing personal appearances along with numerous radio and TV bookings, including a now famous interview on ITV's *This Morning*, with Richard and Judy completely oblivious to the hoax. It helped that Debbie's famous mother was happy to do photo shoots and interviews to get her daughter's pop career off the ground, but there was a problem: despite all the media attention the single wasn't selling and scraped into the chart at number 86.

The first time I felt a bit uncomfortable was when one of the shops that Full Force serviced called to say that somebody had just purchased 15 copies of the record. It was clear that a buying team had been employed which was driving around the country purchasing copies of the record to try and help it climb the chart. It was later revealed that over 800 copies of the record had been bought this way. Alarm bells should have rung when Barry called, asking to meet, as he would like to give me a crate of champagne to thank me and my team for all their efforts. That puzzled me! Barry had paid us a fortune yet the record had peaked at number 86. Still, I wasn't going to turn down a crate of free champagne and agreed to meet Barry in a car park to collect my reward.

When I arrived, he said the champagne was in the boot of the car, but when I opened it to pick up the label on the bottles was 'Perrier' – the crate contained 12 bottles of fizzy water! Before I had a chance to question this a voice boomed behind me, "Dodgy Del, I accuse you of chart hyping!" It was Roger Cook, with a film and lighting crew in tow. I was lost for words as a microphone was thrust into my face. The only thing I could say was "I haven't done anything wrong!" (in a voice 10 octaves higher than normal) as I struggled to answer Roger's questions.

I decided the best course of action was to flee back into the safety of the offices of Full Force. I locked myself in a room and noticed just how much I was shaking while Roger continued to shout questions at me from the street below. My bosses, though understanding, would make no decision on my future until he had seen the programme.

The next few weeks were stressful to say the least. I phoned my parents to ask them if they ever watched *The Cook Report*. "Yes" replied my mum, "it's one of our favourite programmes." I told her that I was going to be in an episode in a couple of weeks' time – she sounded quite proud until I explained that I was referred to as 'Dodgy Del' in the show and was being portrayed as a villain. Soon ITV started showing trailers for the show and Roger Cook proudly announced that in the new series they were investigating paedophiles and arms dealers, and had a two-part show on the people who hype the charts. This was terrible; not only was I being lumped in with paedophiles and arms dealers but the show was going to be shown in *two parts!*

The day of the first broadcast was June 3. I felt sick and was desperately trying to think of what I had said to Barry at the meetings in the pub. The programme started with Roger explaining that the show was about how records could be manipulated into the chart. He finished his introduction by saying that later on they would be meeting this man 'Dodgy Del' whereupon a photo of me filled the TV screen. The tension was unbearable but to my surprise I didn't actually feature until the last two minutes of the show, with Roger surprising me while I took the bottles of Perrier water out of the boot of Barry's car. The programme finished with Roger saying: "In next week's show we'll see what Dodgy Del has to say for himself!" I had another week to wait to see how much trouble I was in.

When the second part of the investigation was shown my revelations were not as bad as I'd expected them to be – it turned out (and the programmed showed) that it wasn't just us; hyping singles had become common practice throughout the music industry and my bosses informed me that my job was safe. It was somewhat ironic, however, that despite revealing some unhealthy practices, *The Cook Report* into the music industry showed that hyping didn't, in fact, work. Despite spending tens of thousands of pounds on promotion, the fact that the Debbie Currie single had only reached the dizzy heights of number 86 showed that the hyping had failed. The mistake *The Cook Report* made was not picking a good record in the first place; if they had, the results may have been different.

As for me, I found myself becoming somewhat of a notorious celebrity as it seemed that half of Tooting, where I was living, had watched the programme. People in the street and in the shops would shout out "Hey, Dodgy Del!" After a few months I decided I needed some respite so I left the music industry and along with my girlfriend, Nicky, bought a camper van and toured the world for a much needed sabbatical.

Jim Henderson, EMI rep

Back in 2010, I was selling in EMI's *An Introduction To Syd Barrett* compilation album when one of my shops asked me (without a hint of irony or sarcasm) whether Syd was touring to promote it "Alas," I explained, "he left this mortal coil in 2006 but he hadn't been active in music since the 1970s!"

The shop's buyer responded, "Oh yes, it's the other one that tours isn't it?" (Presumably he meant David Gilmour, also from Pink Floyd....)

* * *

The worst promotion of a record I came across was from a rival company called Impulse. They were promoting a hip hop single by the band Whistle called 'Just Buggin''. The record had reached number seven in the chart so the reps would go into the record shops and ask the question: "What number is Whistle in the chart?"

"Number seven."

"Where do we want it to go?" shouts the rep.

"Up, I presume!"

The rep would then produce some cans of 7 Up lemonade, the idea being that each time a person drank a can of 7 Up they'd remember the Whistle record...

* * *

One record shop I'll never forget (though I can't remember the name!) was in the West Yorkshire mining town of South Elmsall. The town had a population of less than 7,000 yet for a while sustained a record shop. Most men in the town were employed at Frickley Colliery and I recall that parking outside the shop wasn't a problem as the yellow lines, along with everything else in South Elmsall, was covered in a thin layer of coal dust.

My first visit was in 1986 and following the miners' strikes of 1984 the owner, Gina, said she couldn't afford to buy stock as nobody in the town had any money. In a gesture of support for the miners and to help her out, all the reps decided to still make the journey and give her free stock. This lasted for three years, with the shop surviving totally on gifts from the reps. Eventually the saga of the record shop who never bought records ended when the owner finally shut the doors. She wasn't alone, as due to the devastating effect the strike had on the local community many other businesses closed, too.

* * *

My favourite week at EMI was when I was involved in the big betting coup of 1987. The week before Christmas, bookmakers were predicting 'Fairytale Of New York' by The Pogues and featuring Kirsty MacColl was favourite to be Christmas number one. What the bookmakers hadn't realised was that in 1987 the music industry started producing midweek charts, and that week's midweek chart showed that the Pet Shop Boys 'Always On My Mind' was selling thousands more than The Pogues and was certain to hit the top spot come Christmas. This happened years before Internet betting and EMI employees were driving all over the country, visiting any bookmaker prepared to lay them odds. The staff at EMI collected a huge Christmas bonus that year!

Martin Palmer, former WEA rep, now selling musical instruments in Manchester

In 1986, WEA decided to hold a European conference in Montreux, Switzerland and the UK delegates arrived in a red double-decker London bus. The bus was driven empty from London to Geneva where the delegates had flown the first part of the journey. The bus then meandered through Switzerland on a route designed to miss the low bridges. I remember the journey as a blur due to the large amounts of alcohol consumed. At least one member of the party fell off the open platform of the bus en route to the hotel and had to be picked up from the road before the bus could continue. It's easy to understand the music industry's attitude at this point; CDs were selling for £14 and money was flowing into their coffers, but the land of milk and honey was soon to dry up as an unprepared industry approached the digital age.

* * *

My first job was as a merchandising rep. I had to drive round with a car full of the latest album sleeves, posters and, on occasion, big cardboard cut-outs known as 'centrepieces', all of which were for decorating walls and windows of record shops across the north-west of England. Every major company had either its own merchandising reps, or contractors, all battling for wall space, and the scarcer but more important windows. Armed with an industrial strength staple gun and a reel of nylon line, we built 3-D masterpieces from those sleeves and posters, most of which were destined to stay in place for a couple of days or so at most, until the next rep rolled up with something newer. We were given Polaroid cameras, and had to mail back the evidence of our work every evening. One of the items I remember from those days was a life-size cut-out of singer-songwriter Nick Lowe, to promote his *Jesus Of Coo* album. The cut-out had Nick's right forearm attached to a battery-operated mechanism, which would swing the arm as if he was playing the guitar!

*　　*　　*

I remember doing a personal appearance (PA) with British electronic music outfit 808 State in Manchester. Some genius at Head Office had decided that in order to get the local people excited by the new single we needed to create an opportunity to meet and greet the band.

But come the day and the hour, despite posters and flyers, Virgin Records on Market Street remained unpopulated by rabid 808 State fans, or 808 State themselves. I waited anxiously as the band was 10, then 20 minutes late arriving – not that anyone seemed to be waiting for them anyway, apart from me. Eventually, one of their assistants arrived and asked me if there was anyone around. Quite understandably, they didn't want to make a grand entrance if nobody had turned up. Eventually the band drifted in, mooched around the store and signed a couple of autographs, then mooched off again – no need for the refreshments, the box full of Sharpies or stacks of singles ready to sign. Of course what the London-based marketing whizz-kids had failed to appreciate was that in Manchester we are very laid-back about home-grown talent. Anyone at all interested in 808 State would probably bump into them around town, in Oldham or in Eastern Bloc (the record shop run by the band's Martin Price) and didn't need to turn out to a special event to meet musicians they could run into any day of the week.

*　　*　　*

The most unusual shop I visited was Greaves Records in Rhyl. The owner maintained a shrine to Elvis in a corner at the back of the shop; yes, a proper shrine! It didn't do much for the atmosphere of the shop, in fact they should have renamed it Graves!

Steve Jennings, former EMI and Vital Distribution rep

At Vital Distribution our weekly pre-sale portfolio would range between 50 and 70 different products, both singles and albums. Often this became a problem with busy store owners, managers and buyers when they saw the size of the sales folder and would quickly realise it'd be a task to get through it when they clearly had other things to do. Most of them would inevitably attempt to rush things along so sometimes there was literally a 10-second slot to grab attention for the lower key releases before the page was turned to the next item, usually accompanied with the words "No!" or "We'll leave that one."

To make even the most eclectic release interesting it was important to have your 'script' ready and rehearsed before first call on a Monday morning. An amusing comment could break the ice of the hard facts and figures regarding expected sales, tour dates, *NME* reviews, etc. Sometimes there wasn't a lot of information to work with, maybe just a few lines. I recall one 12″ release, a record by The Eric Kupper Project (pronounced 'Cuppa') on Tribal UK, a house label with origins in the States. We had one line of info and I was definitely not clued up on house music. I was struggling to think of anything interesting to say about the record so I came up with a bit of funny fiction. "Here is the latest release by Tribal UK, one of the growing house labels in the UK. This is a track by 'Eric Cuppa' who is going to team up in the future with Ice-T to create the 'Cuppa-T Project' and, by the way, have you put the kettle on?" Genius! The line was always greeted with a light laugh from those listening and every shop in my region took at least one copy of the title, and I broke the world tea-drinking record in a single week!

But this light-hearted comment, aimed at creating interest in an otherwise low-key release, soon twisted out of control. Word spread that Ice-T was recording for Tribal UK. If true, this was a major industry story as he was one of the biggest artists in the world, and a hip hop, not house, artist at that. This was big news.

Vital's telesales team were asked to confirm if the rumours were true, when would the release date be and would there be an album to follow. Stores in other regions were asking their Vital reps about the release and this was ultimately passed back to the label manager who was obviously clueless to any potential project between Kupper and Ice-T. It was even mentioned at a Vital sales meeting, and I believe that led to a formal denial by the label.

The rumour seemed to linger for ages but eventually it died a death, although I was always more careful with my banter thereafter.

* * *

EMI were always looking for gimmicks to make priority records stand out with store staff to ensure we got our share of 'favours'.

When the Thomas Dolby single 'Hot Sauce' was released, someone in the office came up with the novel idea that all reps should give a bottle of sauce to every store, with a well-placed sticker covering the brand so that artist and title would be highlighted instead, thus ensuring the staff would be thinking about the record even when enjoying their lunchtime fish and chips!

First, every rep had to visit their local supermarket to buy bottles of sauce. I recall the rainy Monday night in 1989 like it was yesterday; I turned up to my local Co-op and bought their entire stock of tomato ketchup and brown sauce as a standalone purchase. The checkout girl looked at my trolley contents, then at me (like I was an alien), then my trolley again before saying "Do you like sauce or something?"

I made a pathetic attempt at beginning to tell her the background of my strange purchase before just giving in and saying "Yes – love the stuff!"

* * *

Traffic wardens were often the nemesis of the record rep, especially where stores were located with no legal parking close to hand. Because we had car stock we felt we were simply delivery drivers, therefore we were allowed to park on single yellow lines or in delivery bays. But we had to take an order first, which sometimes took 30 minutes to an hour to secure, leading many wardens to argue we should park legally, gain the order, deliver our stock and then go on our way. But for some stores you simply had to take the risk or you wouldn't have completed your dozen or so calls for that day.

It appeared that every town or city trained their wardens to be either really nice or complete Rottweilers! In Torquay, for instance, the wardens were always courteous, despite the reps parking illegally. This also applied to the traffic wardens of Cardiff, Bath and Exeter. But in Plymouth, Swansea and Cheltenham it was a completely different story.

There was one leafy market town deep in the New Forest that had a music store with nearest legal parking half a mile away. This town also employed a warden that I shall describe as a battleaxe, even though that is insulting to battle axes – she was horrible! When any record rep's car tyre even touched a yellow line she would appear from nowhere, book in hand, ready to issue a ticket. But she met her match with one south London-based female rep who was more than happy to take her on, and I recall several slanging matches between the two. This particular rep was very attractive and enjoyed to power dress, giving her an obvious advantage with any store's male staff. She decided she would park in the alleyway adjacent to the store even though this meant blocking access to the businesses at the end of the lane. It wasn't illegal to park there and if anybody came into the store to ask her to move she had the smile and the looks to calm the situation immediately.

One particularly wet day I witnessed the power-dressed rep leave the store and walk the 10 yards or so to her car. The aforementioned battleaxe then appeared to 'greet' her and so began their weekly row, with the battleaxe informing the rep she was parked illegally and the rep inviting the battleaxe to go forth and multiply! It was normally quite fun to watch but this day the warden stood in front of the rep's car, refusing to move. The rep started her engine and invited the warden to get out of the way (or words to that effect!) However, she refused so the rep revved her engine loudly and inched her car forward. The warden wouldn't move so the rep inched forward again, making the slightest contact with the battle axe's knee. This was nothing more than a gentle kiss! The warden fell to the ground like a sack of potatoes or a European footballer while grabbing her radio and screaming into it: "Officer down, officer down!"

The rep got out of her car, looked at me and said: "I never touched her!", but before she could finish her sentence a police car came screaming down the street and two burly officers got out, pinning the rep face down on the puddle-filled pavement while pulling her arms behind her back and placing handcuffs on her wrists. The warden was writhing in apparent agony, claiming her leg was broken. Meanwhile the rep, never known for wearing that many clothes, was ungraciously lying in the Hampshire rain with soaked-through T-shirt and mini-skirt ripped to pieces while two policemen pushed down on her to limit her chances of making an escape. I attempted to reason with the officers but was told in colourful language to move along. The rep was then placed in the back of a police car and whisked away for questioning while the warden made a dramatic recovery from her 'broken leg'!

Luckily I wasn't the only witness – in the end there was quite a crowd and no charges were pressed. A week later battleaxe and rep resumed their weekly bouts, but from then on with a bit of additional colour thrown in for good measure.

*　　*　　*

Selling a band's product to any store in or near their hometown was always quite exciting, especially if the band was relatively unknown elsewhere.

There was one such band native to Newport, south Wales, who were immensely popular locally but were never going to challenge Oasis at the top of the charts. Selling the band's new CD and vinyl to the two established record shops in the town was no problem at all but there was a newly opened store, owned and run by people interested only in selling chart product and high-selling back catalogue. When I presented this new release the owner initially turned it down as no one in the store had ever heard of the band. When I stated they were from Newport there came a second refusal with the owner saying: "I don't care, I still haven't heard of them!"

One of the junior staff then asked me if the band was any good and by now I was a little agitated so replied: "No, they're absolute garbage but that doesn't matter because you are going to sell over a hundred copies in the first week!" This statement was met with loud roars of laughter from all store staff. In desperation, I then said I would buy back any stock not sold from the initial pre-order from my own pocket. Job done! The store owner confirmed this unique sale or return agreement and signed up to 110 units as pre-sale and, after release, sold them all in the first four days. They sold the album consistently thereafter as a stock item. Success!

Well, it would have been an amazing success had I paid more attention to who was witnessing my unique sales strategy – none other than the band's manager and father of the lead singer, who was wholly unimpressed with both my 'critique' of the band and the fact that I had to practically sell myself to gain the sale. He complained to the product manager and it was passed to the company MD who left me in no doubt about his thoughts when I was next in the office. My ears are still burning years later!

Does the end justify the means? Not all the time…

* * *

Conferences could be good fun and it was sometimes, but not always, nice to meet the artists, whether established musicians or those just starting their musical careers.

At one EMI conference I recall checking the table plan on my way to dinner to see who I would be sitting with. To my left was some guy called Damon

Albarn. I asked a colleague who this was and he informed me that Mr Albarn was from some group that Food Records had signed called Blur. I introduced myself to him and attempted to make polite, passive conversation about him, his group, his group's forthcoming debut single, the weather – anything that would get him speaking, but to no avail. This was one very quiet gentleman.

At the end of the meal one of the serving staff was taking orders for after-dinner drinks and asked the Blur singer if he would like a liqueur. "A liqueur, what's that?" enquired Damon, to which the server replied: "Port? Brandy?"

Damon then responded: "Yes I'd love a port and brandy, thank you very much!"

*   *   *

A few weeks after I joined EMI the reps were offered a mystery incentive if the Bobby McFerrin single 'Don't Worry, Be Happy' reached the Top five. It peaked at number two so we were all whisked off to Spain for a few days over the first weekend of December 1988, which gave me a great opportunity to meet my new colleagues.

A week before this, Cliff Richard's 'Mistletoe And Wine' had entered the charts at number four and there was much optimism that it would make it to Christmas number one. EMI paid £100 tax free to each rep for every chart-topper and there was normally a gold disc for the bathroom wall. But there was also the glory – it was a great feeling to have one of your records at the top of the charts, regardless of the artist!

After dinner on the Sunday night of this trip the EMI reps were all located in a poorly populated nightclub in Benidorm, awaiting news of the latest chart to see if we'd made it to the top. Remember, these were the days when Radio 1 announced the chart live on air at 7p.m. on a Sunday and phone contact between the UK and Spain was poor at best. We waited nervously for the regional manager to appear with the news. He entered the club very grim faced and ambled across the empty dance floor. He then broke his unhappy look, punched the air and said: "We're number one!"

This prompted much hugging, high-fiving and loud cheering from the group of 'young' reps, which attracted the attention of the DJ and the few other people in the club. The celebrations went on for a fair few minutes and you would have thought we'd won the pools!

Some time later the DJ approached me and asked: "Hey mate, what's the celebration?"

I grinned, punched the air and replied: "Cliff Richard's number one!"

This prompted regular comments from our fellow clubbers of "God loves you," and "You shouldn't be drinking that, the vicar won't like it!"

* * *

The annual EMI conference could be daunting; so many thousand strangers from around the world at one event, meaning you never knew who you were sitting with or talking to.

During one conference at an afternoon presentation I took a seat next to an elegant looking gentleman dressed all in black who, when he introduced himself, was obviously from the USA, such was the strength of his accent. We made passive conversation and he asked me a question. A few months previously EMI had acquired an American based record company for a reported £52 million investment. The American asked for my thoughts on the matter.

"Well," I said, "I wouldn't personally spend 52p on that! I mean, what artists do they have left?" (I promptly named and degraded the four ageing groups left within the portfolio and those that had – in my opinion – the good sense to leave!)

The American looked puzzled. To seal my thoughts I also offered that I thought whoever brokered this deal obviously knows nothing about music or someone is bonking someone in authority.

The conversation ended when the speaker cleared his throat to address the conference. He then announced that there was a special guest in the audience, none other than one of EMI Worldwide's top dogs. The mention of his name prompted loud cheering and applause and the elegant looking gentleman from the USA, sat next to me and dressed all in black, stood up to acknowledge the conference delegates. It is probably no surprise that my EMI career was always destined to be short and eventful...

* * *

You could meet famous people in record shops and sometimes the not-so-obviously-famous. I recall one very poignant meeting with a well-known face while visiting Spillers Records in Cardiff, the world's oldest surviving record shop, on a day around Christmas 1994.

It was particularly busy and the store staff stretched to serve all the customers who were forming a queue four to five people deep at the counter. The manager ushered me into the back, along with a sales assistant, and said, "Richey, will make you a cup of tea?"

I started talking to Richey, who was – I have to say – a very polite and enthusiastic young man. He did indeed make me a cuppa and we probably spoke for 20 minutes or so about football, music and clothes before I was summoned to the counter to present my wares while the manager served customers at the same time.

A few weeks later, well into the New Year, I visited Spillers again and was asked "What did you say to Richey last time you were here?"

"Richey who?" I enquired.

"The guy who made you a cup of tea here before Christmas!" was the reply, "that was Richey Edwards of the Manics!" I didn't have a clue that I had spent such an amount of time with one of the Manic Street Preachers.

But Edwards' face became very recognisable in the weeks, months and years to come after appearing on every newspaper and TV news programme in the UK and beyond because he'd gone missing a few days before my second visit to the shop. In fact, at the time of writing, Richey has never been found and is officially presumed dead.

* * *

I was at Soundz in Paignton one Monday as part of my call plan. In the background a customer was perusing the vinyl album display and had been doing so for about 30 minutes when he approached the owner, Mike, at the counter with an LP in each hand. He held aloft the LP in his left hand, a back catalogue Journey album, retailing at £3.99 as part of a mid-price campaign, and then the album in his right hand, a recently released Metallica LP, retailing at £6.99. He wondered out loud why there was such a disparity in the price of the two albums.

Mike explained that the Journey album was released several years ago and now part of a sale as the record company had lowered the cost price to shift units, whereas the Metallica album was still in the charts so was selling at full price.

Looking perplexed the customer then held up the Metallica album and asked: "So is it likely that this album will one day be lower priced like the Journey album?"

Mike responded: "Yes, it's possible, but that's up to the record company and I can't answer for definite."

The customer (still holding aloft the Metallica LP) asked further: "So when is it likely that the record company will lower the price of this album?"

Mike now looked ruffled and slightly aggravated when he responded: "Well, I don't know. It may be next year, five years' time, ten years' time – any time!"

The customer gave a sideways glance to both albums, turned and placed both back in the racking before responding with "Ok, I'll wait! and leaving the shop.

* * *

Record shop staff always enjoyed tales from the reps after company meetings and conferences, particularly in the South West where we often felt a little off the beaten track and left out.

EMI had an amazing year in 1990 and the company conference was a real celebration with a host of recording artists present. I was in a group of people talking to Neil Tennant from the Pet Shop Boys and felt the wrathful presence of company management when I asked him what he'd thought of reported comments made by U2's Bono in the music press after the Pet Shop Boys had been named Best British Group (the comments were allegedly dismissing the band as a real group). Eventually the management disappeared and I was left alone with Neil, who told me he intended to "get U2 back" by recording an ultra camp disco medley of their single 'Where The Streets Have No Name' and the Boystown Gang's gay anthem 'I Can't Take My Eyes Off You'. I thought this was brilliant!

I knew a lot of Pet Shop Boys fans in my stores so in the following weeks I promptly told them all about my inside information and it didn't take long for word to get out. Every week I was asked for updates on the release date and further questions regarding mixes and remixes. Months passed and, well, nothing on the release schedules and no word from group or management. Any credibility I had was gone. About 7 months after the conference the single's release was finally confirmed and charted in the Top 5 around Easter 1991. I have never been so glad to see a single released! Some credibility restored.

* * *

Local bands would often ask us reps for advice and I got to know quite a few musicians as I ventured to some of the more remote areas, being one of the very few reps that travelled as far as Cornwall every week.

A young indie rock band from Falmouth latched on to me asking for advice on a suitable band name. This was the time of the start of the Premier League in football and the country was still reminiscing about Gazza's efforts in Italia 1990 so there were groups popping up with names like Eusebio, Pelé, Sultans of Ping FC and, I recall, the Milltown Brothers promoting themselves with replica shirts featuring their beloved Burnley FC. As this young Cornish band were all football fans, I suggested a football theme and they agreed.

I continued my unpaid consultancy by offering a few options, such as Rivaldo, Ronaldo, Cruyff, Inter, Bayern, Borussia and Rovers, to name but a few. The band went away to consider their options and did decide football could provide a suitable name. Unfortunately, I don't think the band Halifax Town FC was ever going to take the music industry by storm…

* * *

A rep's company car was his office and a mini warehouse, too. It was important to have the boot neatly laid out so car stock orders could be honoured quickly and efficiently and you could see which titles were running low. I was one of many who purchased plastic boxes of differing sizes so that vinyl, CDs and tapes were readily available, since cardboard did have a habit of breaking, which could damage vinyl product in particular.

When I first joined Vital Distribution it could be said a large percentage of our portfolio was non-mainstream, specialist, eclectic, i.e. not to everyone's taste.

One of our northern reps endured a theft while his car was parked in his own drive one night. The thieves had broken the rear window, opened the boot and removed all of his car stock. Their job was made easier by the fact that the rep used plastic boxes like myself so all they had to do was transfer several boxes into their own vehicle and head off. The theft was reported the next morning.

A few days later the aforementioned rep was bewildered when he arrived home after a day on the road to find that the thieves had actually returned the car stock to his drive, minus the plastic boxes! Clearly the music on the car that week was not deemed worthy of keeping, even if it was technically free.

* * *

I was visiting PR Sounds in Devizes in my early days at EMI. The store was empty except for a man standing at the counter with a WEA folder in front of him. I had never met the local WEA rep before, so introduced myself and added: "Who are you with mate?" to which he obviously replied WEA.

"What's the big release for you lot this week?" I added and he informed me they were pushing the first single from a band called The Beloved. I decided to offer my opinion: "Good luck with that, I've heard the track and have to say it's shit!"

The gentleman smiled. We were then joined by store manager Roger and another guy, both carrying hot drinks. Roger duly handed one to the gentleman I'd been speaking with. Roger then asked if I knew the two guys and introduced the chap who'd been helping him make drinks as Mike from WEA and the guy I'd been talking to as Jon… from The Beloved…

* * *

I wasn't really a local celebrity in my hometown in Devon, but people did know I worked in the industry and my job was deemed more glitzy and glamorous than the mainstream jobs most of my friends had. This did prompt some attention from locals all wanting to know who the next big thing was going to be. There are still those who mention to me even now that I had 'predicted' that Oasis would be huge – same for Elastica, the Manic Street Preachers and other chart-topping singles, all predictions made well before the artist or product was in the charts. I was generally known to be 'in the know', even if the predictions were rather obvious and not exactly breaking news.

Just before Christmas 1994 the local paper contacted me to ask my opinion on who would be Christmas number one as they had found out that I lived locally and worked in the trade. The hot favourite was East 17 but I decided not to go for the obvious one and opted for 'Whatever' by Oasis, but did state it was a long shot. The paper printed my quote but decided against the 'long shot' disclaimer. East 17 did duly take the number one spot and Oasis, having been number two on the midweek chart, entered at number three. The next three months or so I spent fending off angry comments from friends and associates all informing me they had seen the paper and promptly placed considerable cash on Oasis, especially when they saw the odds were 20/1 or so. How could I be wrong, I was 'in the know' when it came to all things music? I never knew people took me so seriously!

* * *

The great thing about being a rep in the music industry was that we didn't have to wear suits and could have long hair if we wanted. While I worked at EMI I went through a 'rock' period where my hair was very long and I wore faded jeans with various rips and slashes as standard. But that wasn't always so great.

One day I was travelling between Devizes and Marlborough in my Vauxhall Carlton estate when I spotted a police car approaching behind, so slowed down to the appropriate speed limit. I could see in my rear view mirror that the passenger was on the police radio and he was dictating my number plate. After two or three minutes the car overtook me and sped off. A few miles along the road the same police car was parked in a lay-by and promptly pulled out behind me as I passed. Once again the passenger was deeply preoccupied with his radio and obviously something about my car or me had gained his attention. Again they overtook, with both policemen looking curiously at me before heading off. Once more a few miles up the road they were parked and pulled out behind me as I passed. I'd had enough. At the next lay-by I pulled in and got out of my car and the police car pulled in behind me, both officers getting out.

"Can I help you officers?" I asked before one responded in a broad Welsh accent.

"Now what would you be doing in a car like this sonny?"

"I work as a rep!" I replied. This prompted loud laughter from both officers.

"Dressed like that?" one shouted through his laughter.

"Yes, I work for a record company!" I responded. This prompted even louder laughter.

"You work for a record company? I've heard it all now. If that's true my name is Paul McCartney!"

I held my hand out: "Pleased to meet you Mr McCartney!" You can imagine the response was far more threatening than previous as my attempt at humour was not well received. I opened my boot to show the car stock. This did not have the desired effect.

"My god, you have been busy sonny! Where did you get all this stuff?" one asked. His face was beaming, as though he had just caught the great train robber or something!

"I told you – I work for a record company!" I said, and held out my company card. I was informed that if I maintained my story and didn't tell the truth then I would be getting intimate with both officers' boots.

I asked them to call the number on the card if they didn't believe me. They used the police radio and, after what seemed like hours, I was asked for my driving licence. The two officers had a short conference and one approached me: "Looks like you got away with it this time sonny!"

I didn't argue, just got in my car and headed off. I did, of course, enjoy a police escort all the way into Marlborough.

Maybe having long hair, being in your twenties and driving a Vauxhall Carlton is a deadly combination!

Phil Day, Warner rep

I was invited to a promotion night which was being held on the set of *Coronation Street* at Granada Studios in Manchester and was hosted by Warner Bros. There were various artists in attendance, including Irish pop band The Corrs and Chris Rea. Everybody knew that Chris was a big fan of motor racing, especially Ferrari. An area manager from Warner Bros. stopped Chris as he entered and presented him with a piece of metal, which was once part of a Ferrari, mounted on a mahogany base on behalf of some Ferrari garage in Scotland. Then he went into a long, boring speech before passing the 'trophy' to Chris who seemed more embarrassed than delighted with it. I recollect the metal/mahogany contraption was left behind on the set.

* * *

During a speech my boss described us as the 'Crème de Menthe' of sales teams. We took it as a compliment as we guessed that what he really meant was the 'Crème de la Crème'…

6

Tales from other music retail-related folk

Have you got...?

Sitting On The Back Of A Duck	('Sitting On The Dock Of The Bay', Otis Redding)
Daft As A Brush	('Thick As A Brick', Jethro Tull)
Central Heating	('Sexual Healing', Marvin Gaye)
Come A Chameleon	('Karma Chameleon', Culture Club)
Slade's The King And I	('Your Love Is King', Sade)
Joey Davison's 'Love Will Tear Us Apart'	('Love Will Tear Us Apart', Joy Division)
Up The Back Passage	('Up The Junction', Squeeze)
Never Mind The Sex, Where Is The Bollocks?	(*Never Mind The Bollocks*)

The Jam singing about 'Going Underground to the Tube Station at Midnight'

A tale from an anonymous security guard at a High Street record shop

I was assigned to work at a small branch in a provincial town. The record chain had run a bonus scheme for the managers, with a massive cash prize for the person who increased the percentage of sales the most over a six-month period. One particular manager was streaking away from the competition and the reason was down to his sales of 'blue' movies.

He had been approached by a sales representative from a video company, asking if the shop would stock his product. The manager looked through his catalogue and said there was no way a reputable company like his would ever stock such product. The rep argued that not all the videos in the catalogue were porn movies; many could be regarded as soft porn. He explained the huge margins that could be made and it got the manager thinking about the bonus scheme. After much persuasion he agreed to give the videos a chance. He took the view that the shop was not in a city and it was very rare that anybody from Head Office paid him a visit. The area manager called in every couple of months to spend a day, but always gave plenty of warning of his impending arrival. Furthermore, the video department was downstairs in the basement, away from the music sections upstairs, which made it an even more tempting proposition.

The next week his first box of videos arrived and like anybody who knows how to market product, he displayed them on the top shelf. Over the next few weeks the videos sold really well, resulting in the manager buying even more stock. With the massive profit margin they were making the store was miles ahead in the bonus scheme competition. He decided to dedicate the top two shelves in the video department to the 'blue' videos. He was also beginning to push his luck as some of the new titles he had taken on were venturing into dangerous territory.

One day I called the manager over and asked him to come to the basement with me. After we descended the stairs I asked the manager if he'd noticed anything unusual. "What do you mean?" he replied. I then pointed out that although the video department was quite busy, every single customer was male and over 50. Many of the men wore flat caps and raincoats. I took a few titles off the top shelf and asked if a reputable chain should be stocking titles such as *Saturday Night Beaver*, *Breast Side Story* and *On Golden Blonde*. The manager agreed. He told me that all the videos were on sale or return and he would send them all back the next month.

"Why not now?" I asked.

"If we sent them back now we might not win the bonus scheme so I just want to keep them for one more month!" said the manager.

A few days later the manager received a phone call from one of his mates at another shop in the chain. "I thought I'd better tip you off that the area manager is on his way to see you. He's planning a surprise visit to see why you're doing so well. He left about half an hour ago!" It would take about 40 minutes to drive between the two shops so the area manager would be arriving in 10 minutes! Mass panic ensued as the manager started boxing up all the porn videos from the shelves. If the AM found out what he was up to he would surely face the sack. He decided the safest place to hide the stash was in the ladies' toilet, but it was only a tiny space and soon the boxes of videos filled the room to the ceiling. He locked the door from the inside, climbed out of the small window, then dropped down on to the car park at the back of the shop. As he walked around to the front he bumped into the AM. They made their way into the shop together, chatting about how well the shop was doing. The AM then asked for a tour of the shop to see what promotions were running. Down in the basement the first thing he noticed was that the top shelves were completely bare. "What's going on here?" he asked. The by now rather flustered manager attempted to fob him off by explaining that he was about to do a new promotion. Suddenly he was interrupted by the shop's only female member of staff.

"I've been waiting to use the toilet for ages but somebody's in there."

"Oh, the door is just stuck I think," replied the manager. "I'll come down and fix it in a minute."

This answer left the girl unimpressed and she stressed to the manager that she desperately needed to go. He suggested she nip over the road and use the toilet in the pub. Then the AM piped up with a suggestion: why not all go down together and force the door open?

Just then another staff member grabbed the AM – he was needed for a phone call. Talk of being saved by the bell! Spying his chance, the manager pleaded with his female assistant to nip quickly over to the pub – he'd owe her one and would explain all later. When the AM returned he asked if the toilet issue had been sorted. "No problem!" came the reply.

The next day the shop returned their stock of porn movies. Not only did they get away with it, but they managed to win the most improved shop in the chain scheme and the crafty manager was rewarded with a huge bonus.

* * *

The following incident happened when I moved to a larger city centre store. I had become wary of the assistant manager and suspected he was bringing drugs on to the premises. I informed the shop's manager and they agreed to do a search of his locker. To their great disappointment they found a substantial bag of white powder, which turned out to be cocaine. Bringing drugs into the shop would result in instant dismissal but the manager was a kind man and offered his AM two options: either he would sack him and call the police or he could tip the cocaine down the toilet and hand in his resignation. All three of them made their way to the toilet and tipped the white powder down the pan. The AM handed in his resignation and left the store. They thought that was the end of the matter, but they were wrong.

The next day a young man strode rather purposely and with a certain amount of aggression into the store. I suspected he wasn't in the shop to buy a new CD and thought it may be wise to follow him. When the young man reached the counter he demanded to see the manager. The assistant asked him to hang on while he went to fetch the manager, who came out of his office to offer his help. But the young man didn't respond. Instead, he swung a punch! It turned out the cocaine we'd tipped down the toilet the previous day belonged to him. Luckily the manager managed to get his chin out of the way. At that point myself and the shop's other security guard grabbed the young man and attempted to escort him out of the shop. The young man lashed out, kicking and throwing punches. We decided to escort him out of the rear of the shop to shield the customers from the fracas. After a mammoth struggle, the young man was removed from the shop, still kicking and screaming. It wasn't a great move on his part, taking on two burly blokes and needless to say he came off worst.

When I returned to the shop one of the assistants asked me if I knew the man. "No idea," I said.

It turned out that the man was in fact a well-known local actor.

"Make-up will be working overtime on him next time he appears on the set, then!" I said.

The tempestuous local actor went on to become a big Hollywood star and each time I see him on TV I think of his unfortunate run-in with us.

Proper tales from me – Graham Jones

As you may know, I co-founded Proper Distribution and in that time I've come across my fair share of strange requests and record shop tales.

In the winter of 2006, the Devon-based folk singer and instrumentalist Seth Lakeman released the album *Freedom Fields*. Seth had the idea to launch the album at the Dartmoor Brewery in Princetown. And what a great idea it was; excellent music, free food and quality beer – it promised to be a memorable evening.

As I knew he was a fan of Seth and and even a bigger fan of food and beer, I invited Keith from Upbeat Records in Bude over to the event. On the evening of the launch the weather was atrocious and I had an arduous journey across the moors in driving snow to reach the venue. Due to the appalling weather it was clear some people hadn't been able to make it. I looked for Keith and assumed he, too, had decided not to risk the drive.

Despite the lower turn-out the evening was a great success, with Seth playing a rocking set. Towards the end I took a call on my mobile – it was Keith. He was not a happy bunny. "I've been in this pub for 2 hours and there's nobody here except two old guys playing dominoes. Are you and Seth going to turn up?" I asked where he was. He was sitting in the Dartmoor Inn, just a little walk away, but the gig was at the Dartmoor Brewery. I rushed over to the pub to get Keith. He greeted me with details of his horrendous journey and his even worse hunger. We got back to the Dartmoor Brewery just in time to hear Seth Lakeman finish his second encore and go on to thank everybody for being a smashing audience. I thought maybe I could get Keith some food, but no such luck as there was nothing left and the staff had tidied the plates away. Instead, I tried to console him with a bag of salted peanuts, but by now he was truly cheesed off. I suggested we could maybe have a curry but trying to get a curry in Princetown at 11.15 on a Monday night proved beyond us. I thanked Keith for coming, wished him a safe journey and hoped he found an open garage so he could satisfy his hunger on the way home.

* * *

A Chinese man with limited English called to say that he was opening a record shop in Cambridge and asked if we could supply him. I explained that we stock over 40,000 different lines and I could send him a file showing the range, but it would probably take him a day to read it. Perhaps he'd let me know what kind of music he was stocking and I could target that particular genre. When he said he was only interested in 'vile records', I burst out laughing and commented that most of the records we stocked were great, some not so good and maybe a few were, in fact, vile. There was a long silence at the end of the phone. Suddenly the penny dropped: we distribute a thrash metal label called Peaceville and the catalogue numbers for their stock starts with the four-letter code 'VILE'. "Sorry, I realise what you want is the Peaceville label!"

"Are they vile records?" came the response.

"Yes they are thrash metal VILE!"

"But I just don't want thrash metal vile records, I want all vile records!" a somewhat exasperated Chinese man shouted down the phone. Another silence followed before it finally clicked – he wasn't asking for vile records, but VINYL records! Silly me!

* * *

BBC North East approached me to do a piece about how people buy music these days. I thought it best to do some market research so I positioned myself outside the HMV shop in Northumberland Street, Newcastle, and approached the great Geordie public…

The first gentleman was aged about 30:

Me:	"Excuse me sir, can you tell me when you last bought music?"
Man:	"About 2 minutes ago!"
Me:	"What format was it – a CD, an LP or a download?"
Man:	"None, it was an LDV."
Me (looking puzzled):	"Where did you buy this LDV?"
Man:	"HDV!" he then turned around and pointed at the shop behind me.

The penny dropped. He had bought a DVD from HMV!

A few minutes later I asked a woman passing by the same question.

Woman: "Oooh I haven't bought music for a long time pet!" she said. "It's not that I don't like music, I do, in fact I love it! The thing is I just don't love it as much as butter!"

I don't know how I was meant to respond to this answer, but I just burst out laughing.

This is my favourite from a 50-year-old gentleman.

Me: "Excuse me sir, can you tell me when you last bought music?"

Gentleman: "About 2 weeks ago."

Me: "What format was it – CD, LP or download?"

Gentleman: "It was an LP."

Me: "What do you like about vinyl?"

Gentleman: "If you spill something on vinyl it doesn't stain and you can wipe it clean, plus it's much easier to lay than carpet!"

For some reason the gentleman had assumed the conversation had moved on to vinyl flooring!

About the author

Graham Jones was born in Anfield, Liverpool. After leaving school he worked in numerous dead-end jobs before getting his first break in the music industry thanks to a colleague's failed comical suicide attempt. Ever the optimist, Graham managed The Cherry Boys – a band that made *Spinal Tap* look mundane – and ran his own market stall, selling vinyl fruit bowls made from Beatles LPs melted into shape under a grill. He eventually found his vocation travelling the country selling records, tapes and CDs. He spent over 20 years of his life visiting and selling to independent record stores and became increasingly disturbed by the sheer volume of shops closing. In 2008, he toured the country and interviewed 50 record shop owners about their lives in music. Those interviews became the basis of his first book *Last Shop Standing (Whatever Happened To Record Shops?)*. The book still continues to sell well, has been updated and is now on its fifth edition. In 2012, Blue Hippo Media turned the book into a film, *Last Shop Standing, The Rise, Fall And Rebirth Of The Independent Record Shop*. The film featured a huge cast of musicians, including Paul Weller, Johnny Marr, Richard Hawley, Norman Cook, Nerina Pallot and Billy Bragg, along with many interviews with the record shop owners. The film received rave reviews and in 2013 was chosen as the 'Official Film of World Record Store Day 2013'. Graham is one of the founders of Proper Music Distribution, the largest independently owned music distribution company in the UK. He can be contacted via the website www.lastshopstanding.com or by email at graham@lastshopstanding. co.uk

About the cartoonist

Kipper Williams's cartoons have appeared in music publications including Melody Maker, Smash Hits and the Black Sabbath World Tour programme (1977). He now draws for the Guardian, The Sunday Times and the Spectator and exhibits and sells his original artwork at the Chris Beetles Gallery in London.

Acknowledgments

Special thanks go to Anna Wood for all her patience in editing the book and Malcolm Mills and all the team at Proper for their support.

I would like to thank all the record shop staff both past and present for all the anecdotes and strange requests they have given me over the years, along with the people listed below for helping me complete this book.

Alan Levermore, Anthony Herschell, Barry Everard, Ben Jones, Chris Charlesworth, Craig Dawson, Danny Vogel, Dave Pike, Dave Sinclair, Gary Farrow, Gennaro Castaldo, Geoff Davis, Glen Ward, Gordon Montgomery, Ian de-Whitell, Ian Grenfell, Jim Henderson, Jon Abnett, Julia Weir, Karl Tierney, Katherine Cooper, Keith Hudson, Lee Wright, Lucy Beevor, Martin Palmer, Martin Nudes, Michael Masters, Mike Houzamdone, Mike Summers, Murray Allan, Neil Sheasby, Noala White, Paul Quirk, Phil Barton, Phil Day, Rachael Rebecca, Rachel Welch, Richard Strange, Rick Lister, Rod Emms, Simon Dullenty, Simon Hibberd, Steve Jennings, Steve Oliver and all the team at That's Entertainment, Steve Redmond, Terry Doyle, William Maneklow.

I would like to end the book by thanking my Mum and Dad, who had they not produced me this book would not exist.

LAST SHOP STANDING

THE BOOK

THE DVD

Last Shop Standing lifts the lid on an area of the music industry in tatters – a sad but true tale of the decline of record shops and their beloved vinyl too. The author, Graham Jones has worked at the heart of the record industry since the golden 1980s. He was there during the fruitful retail years and has witnessed the tragic decline of a business blighted by corruption and corporate greed.

> *"A Great read full of wonderful stories and loads of laughs"*
> **- Johnnie Walker**

> *"A must read book for record collectors and music fans everywhere"*
> **- Record Collector**

> *"Enjoy this humorous and very revealing truth about the record industry"*
> **- Suzie Quatro**

Last Shop Standing, inspired by the book of the same name by Graham Jones, takes you behind the counter to discover why nearly 2000 record shops have already disappeared across the UK. The film charts the rapid rise of record shops in the 1960s / 70s and 80s, the influence of the chart, the underhand deals, the demise of vinyl and rise of the CD as well as new technologies.

Where did it all go wrong?
Why were 3 shops a week closing?
Will we be left with no record shops with the continuing rise of downloading?

Hear from over 20 record shop owners and music industry leaders as well as musicians including Paul Weller, Johnny Marr, Norman Cook, Billy Bragg, Nerina Pallot, Richard Hawley and Clint Boon as they all tell us how the shops became and still are a part of their own musical education, a place to discover and cherish new bands, new music and why they might just have a brighter future.

Available from independent record shops and from